Silent No More:
A Christian Response To Suicide

John Potter

ISBN: 979-8-9867194-1-2

Contents

CHAPTER 1
INTRODUCTION

Suicide is a destructive force that continues to wreak havoc and calamity in our world. Its impact is felt around the entire globe. Over 800,000 people die by suicide each year, according to the World Health Organization (WHO) (2019). More people are dying from suicide than in all of the armed conflicts, wars, and natural disasters worldwide (Schlein 2014). While these numbers are alarming, suicidal behavior is even worse. For each reported suicide, there are more than twenty suicide attempts (WHO 2019). The United States of America is facing its own suicide crisis. According to the National Center for Health Statistics, suicide claimed the lives of 48,344 people in 2018 (Drapeau 2018, 1). American suicides are now at their highest point in fifty years, and they are now the second-leading cause of death for Americans under the age of thirty-five (Keller 2018). Any way one looks at it, suicide is a major issue that deserves our attention and effort to save people's lives.

Individuals with suicidal thoughts often report feelings of being helpless, hopeless, and worthless (LivingWorks 2014, 7). They feel isolated and alone. They talk about being a burden to others. They often employ unhealthy coping mechanisms, like alcohol, drug use, or other risk-taking behaviors. They withdraw from friends and family because of the uncontrollable pain they experience. People at risk of suicide often see a future with endless days of pain, sadness, or suffering. This vision for the future looks nothing like the one they want or would enjoy. They consider suicide as the best way or the only way to escape the hurt of their current situation. Too many people see suicide as the answer to making their pain stop.

The problem of suicide is further exacerbated by the societal response. Suicide is still a hidden or taboo topic, making denial, secrecy, and avoidance common. This is problematic because denying or avoiding a person with thoughts of suicide can be just as deadly as an execution. There is often little willingness to engage the topic or the hurting people who hold thoughts of suicide. Others want to avoid any discussion of suicide because of the stigma and pain that

4

surrounds the issue. There is also a growing attitude in our culture that does not want to address suicide because it is viewed as a private matter, one wherein suicide is considered a personal choice that may be right for the individual. This *laissez-faire* approach has only increased the acceptance and facilitation of suicide as an option for those who consider ending their own lives.

In *Dying of Despair* (2017), Aaron Kheriaty outlines a multitude of modern issues that increase despair. The retreat from marriage, the rise of broken relationships, greater isolation, the loss of social support, and declining religious participation can all be seen as overarching risk factors toward suicide. Kheriaty says that "As a consequence of these changes, many Americans have 'lost the narratives of their lives'" (23). Social fragmentation is also a key factor in suicide. Those who are disconnected are not seeking help, support, or care. People are more isolated and alone than prior generations, and levels of isolation and loneliness continue to rise. Since the 1980s, reported loneliness among adults in the United States increased from twenty percent to forty percent. The recently retired surgeon general announced last year that social isolation is a major public health crisis, on par with heart disease or cancer (22).

Conditions are ripe for Christian communities to engage this hurting population with compassion and concern. The grim statistics should wake congregations from their slumber and silence on suicide. Churches have not responded sufficiently with the biblical, theological, ethical, or congregational approach that people need. Our world desperately needs a Christian voice and perspective to combat suicide through the life, hope, and example of Jesus. Churches seem to take two approaches to suicide. The first is to regard suicide as an entirely secular issue that requires resources and support outside of the church. Terrain where the church once gave support, comfort, and community is yielded wholly to medical methods and scientific treatments. The perceived superiority of psychiatry, psychology, and pharmacology have displaced the church's pastoral response and responsibility to care for hurting people in our communities. The second approach is to exclude medical, psychiatric, psychological, and therapeutic methods and treatments. Some churches, embracing a naïve Biblicism wherein scripture alone can resolve any and every illness, view medicine and science as unnecessary or inappropriate. Suicide is strictly a spiritual matter. This approach emphasizes a spiritual necessity and completely ignores the physical. Here, churches have developed a subtle Gnosticism as it relates to caring for people. They treasure the spiritual but consider the physical treatments of today to be an obstacle. This has led many to reject the physiological needs of depressed individuals and champion only spiritual health needs. A third approach is greatly needed, one that is integrative of scripture as well as the sciences. To address suicide, churches need to embrace the physical, mental, and spiritual aspects of our humanity.

In reality, churches should be the first place to address mental health and suicidal concerns in a community. Clergy act as pastoral counselors for millions of Americans. Christian beliefs are especially influential in the United States, with 70.6% of the country identifying as Christian (Cooperman, 2018). Indeed, according to the American Psychiatric Association Foundation (APAF), "Religion and spirituality often play a vital role in healing, people experiencing mental health concerns often turn first to a faith leader" (2016, 2). Clergy should be viewed as mental health workers on the front line of battle with suicide, because they help people combat suicide every day. The National Institute of Mental Health Epidemiological Catchment Area surveys, reported by Harold Koenig (1998), show that a person with a "mental health diagnosis is more likely to seek assistance from clergy than from psychologists and psychiatrists combined." The frequent use of clergy should not be a surprise, given their availability, accessibility, and the high trust that Americans have in them (350). Clergy are in a good place for long-term relationships with individuals and their families. This enables them to observe changes in behavior that may indicate early signs of distress. Due to the high levels of trust and use, pastors and religious leaders can directly benefit communities that engage those with a mental health diagnosis. Clergy are also caring spiritual leaders who focus on humane and thoughtful treatment of others, as the APAF highlights:

> They provide for the spiritual development and care of their congregations. Faith leaders encounter individuals with mental health conditions in a number of circumstances that require different approaches. They are always called to see the person rather than the illness first, and to understand their own religious

assumptions regarding the role of the divine in their encounters with others. (2016, 15)

Clergy and congregations are perfectly positioned to engage this national crisis.

The church has something to offer hurting people who are prone to suicide. Studies repeatedly show that faith, religion, and spiritual practices are strong protective factors against suicide. People who have faith and practice their faith are less likely to end their life by suicide. They also have stronger coping skills and resiliency and show posttraumatic growth from past trials and difficulties. We now have a sizable body of research that suggests prayer, faith, participation in a religious community, and the practices of cultivating gratitude, forgiveness, and other virtues can reduce the risk of depression, lower the risk of suicide, diminish drug abuse, and aid in recovery (Koenig 1998, 24). Religion and spiritual practices need greater depth and exposure to unleash their powerful healing effects. These practices are able to help people today just as they have in days past. True hope cannot be delivered by a medical prescription or a therapy session. The church must unleash the story of Christ to bring healing and recovery.

Suicide is more than a public health threat; it is a cry for help. The sad, the lonely, and the suffering want something more than what they can find in this world. Jesus can speak to their needs. Loving and compassionate people are now required to stand in the gap and support those at risk of suicide. The Christian faith through scripture, spiritual practices, and congregational care can combat suicide. In addition to these aids, Christians believe that God directly works in and through their lives, providing needed comfort, encouragement, guidance, and strength. Just as Christians believe that God's grace aids them for salvation, they believe that God's Holy Spirit aids all who struggle with the prospect of suicide.

Medical and mental health providers seem ready to welcome religion and faith leaders back into a community approach where together they can address suicide. Churches, congregations, and clergy should continue to move in the same direction. Caretakers of the body, mind, and soul can make a huge difference, if they are willing to work together – and they should work together.

An integrative approach is needed to combat suicide, bringing the most productive outcome for people who are struggling to stay alive. The church can reflect Jesus by resuming this role. I believe that it is up to the task of providing hope, love, and life in our society. If we will end our silence on suicide, then we can connect hurting people with the Savior and Redeemer of the world.

Mission Statement

This book will examine the role of scripture, spiritual practices, and local congregations as tools with which to address suicide. Although suicide involves multiple physiological, psychological, and cultural factors, Christians can provide holistic help to those at risk of suicide as a way of ministering to their needs.

Focus Questions

1) What factors reduce suicide?

2) What does scripture teach regarding suicide?

3) How have spiritual practices been used among people at risk of suicide?

4) What spiritual practices are most helpful against suicide?

5) How can local congregations support people at risk of suicide?

Methodology

The methodology for this book will incorporate multiple approaches. A textual approach will examine what scripture says about suicide. I will also examine the seven suicides listed in scripture and suicidal statements found in scripture. This is not a biblical studies project per se, but I consider historical and critical issues when they are applicable. Biblical commentaries and other scholarly references will be used to interpret key texts pertaining to suicide. Other Christian texts I will investigate include theological and ministry sources, especially those that contribute insights in aiding those who struggle with the prospect of suicide.

In addition, I will integrate behavioral scientific studies and research from several journals, papers, and articles on suicide. For example, quantitative and qualitative investigations reveal factors that impact suicide, resiliency, and post-traumatic growth.

Finally, a theoretical approach will offer constructive ways that the theological and empirical implications can address suicide. The integration of biblical and behavioral scientific data will help Christians become more empathetic, expert, and effective in how churches minister to those at risk of suicide.

Integration

Since this project will incorporate physiology, psychology, and theology, it is important to discuss how I integrate them. These are three separate and distinct disciplines, but each provides unique knowledge that is beneficial to address suicide. The knowledge of these three fields is important to all human beings because of how we are made. I suggest that scripture advocates an anthropology wherein humans exist in a unity of three parts or aspects.

Scripture describes us as a three-part being, each part affecting the others.[1] God has created humanity with the distinctness of a physical body, a mind, and a spirit (Deut. 6:4-5; Mark 12:30; Rom. 12:1-2; 1 Cor. 14:15; 2 Cor. 5:1-8; 1 Thes. 5:23).[2] Matthew Stanford (2008) concurs that "We are complex beings, unlike any other living creature: the union of a physical body with an immaterial mind and spirit. While each aspect is separate, in some sense, they are connected and affect one another" (5).[3] The body, mind, and spirit are important because God created us as a unity of these three parts. We exist in a physical body to interact with the world around us. The mind allows us to think, decide, and choose. It controls our actions, mental processes, and behaviors. The spirit is representative of our inmost being. People can be said to consist of the very breath of God placed in a dusty shell (Gen. 2:7). Again, we are not just a sack of cells but, rather, an inbreathed spirit of God's own unique design. We are a living spirit, much more than a living body. The spirit signifies our true eternal essence and identity, not our outward tent of skin (2 Cor. 5:1). Stanford continues, "It is in our spirit that we have the opportunity to be in union with the very God of the universe (Proverbs 20:27; Romans 8:16)" (Stanford, 10). Be that as it may, people's body – their physical, material self – is inextricably bound up with the whole of who they are. Just as God described the creation of people, including their body, as being "good" (Gen. 1), and just as people's salvation includes the resurrection of their body (1 Cor. 15) along with everything else, people cannot be wholly understood by considering only one part of them. Stanford illustrates:

> "It is in our mind that we choose to sin (2 Corinthians 10:5); and it is with our body (Ephesians 2:3), or 'members' (Romans 7:23), that we act out our sinful thoughts. This process is altered only in the individual who comes to a saving faith in Christ Jesus, and even then, that believer continues to struggle with a sinfully programmed mind and body (Romans 7:14-25)." (13-14)

The unity of our three aspects shows how they interact with each other. In Paul's letter to the Colossians, he encourages them: "Set your mind on the things above, not on the things that are on earth" (3:2). We have freedom in where we set the mind. Paul declares that the people of God should practice a new way of living and thinking, one that focuses on the new and better way of Jesus. It is here where people can build their life upon the love and example of Jesus. We must practice "taking every thought captive to the obedience of Christ" (2 Cor. 10:5). This allows people to concentrate on the better things of God and avoid common temptations. When we set our minds in a different direction from that of the world, we "do not give the devil an opportunity" (Eph. 4:27). If we resist wrong thinking, there is no foothold for temptation to establish within us. Paul tells the Roman church to "be transformed by the renewing of your mind, so that you may prove what the will of God is, that which is good and acceptable and perfect" (Rom. 12:2). The renewed mind helps people to live in a better way, the righteous way of Jesus. Scripture advocates a body, mind, and spirit approach for us to follow. All three aspects of the self are connected and require our attention in pursuing wellness.

Figure 1 represents the three-part being of humanity, without denying the holistic nature of who people are. The figure shows three concentric circles that constitute our body, mind, and spirit. Each part is drawn separately but interacts with the ones above and or below it. The outer circle is the body and is in contact with the mind. The middle circle is the mind. It is connected to the body through functions of the brain and our nervous system but also with the spirit. The spirit, when connected to God, works to transform the mind into the image of Christ, which results in an increasing display of godly behaviors through the physical body (Stanford 2008, 10-11).

Figure 1.

Three-Part Being of Humanity

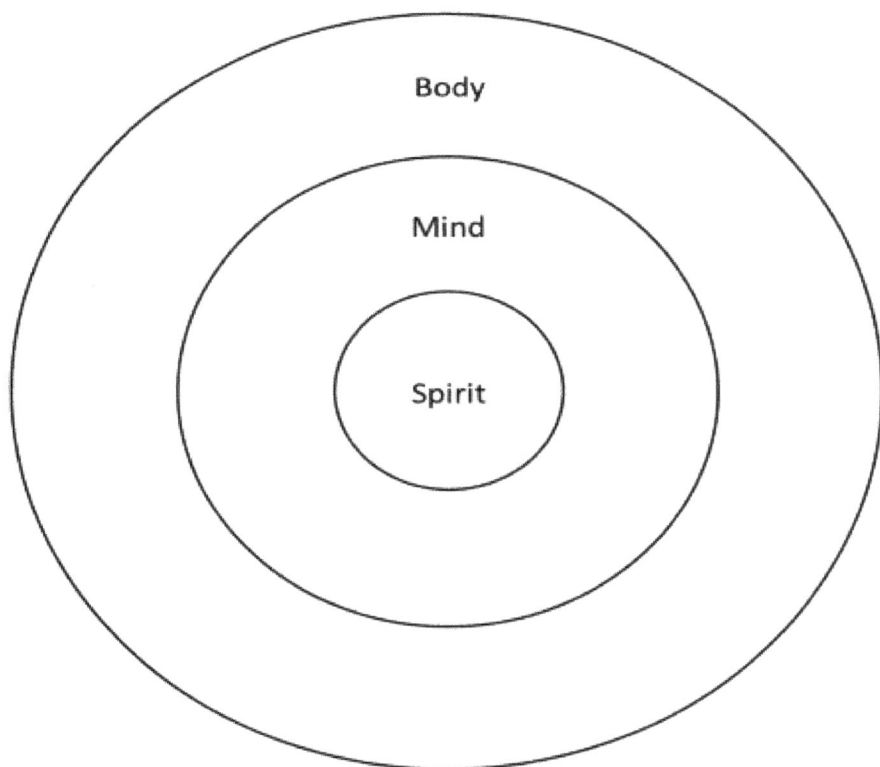

Dallas Willard uses a similar figure to diagram "his understanding of the interlocking and interdependent aspects of the 'person' or the self" (Black 2013, 99). In Figure 2, Willard highlights that scripture captures a variety of ways to describe our inner being. He uses terms like *spirit*, *heart*, and *will* to reflect how God has created us with more than a mind and body. Willard, too, leans on scripture to identify an anthropology of humans being formed as a unity of different aspects. He also shows that there is a richness and complexity to our humanity. We are not just flesh and blood, rather, our components reflect something greater than our physical bodies. Willard understands that the aspects of the self may not be entirely obvious to us at first, but they are not intended to be mysterious (Black, 100). Willard argues that "God is not interested in 'hiding' the essential things of life and living. In fact, the opposite is true. God has created all things in ways and through means that can be discerned and intelligently approached as to gather increasing understanding" (Willard, 100).

Figure 2.

The Whole Person

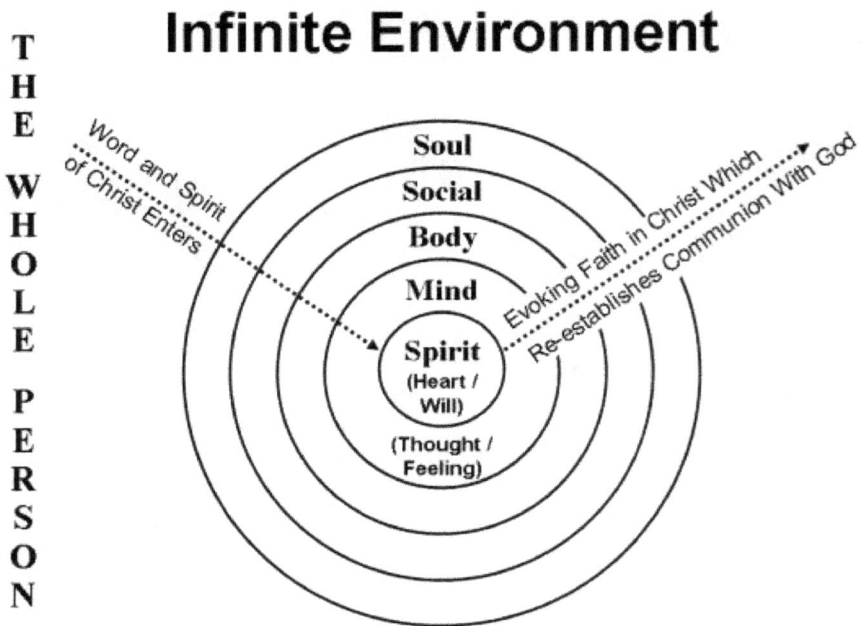

(Willard, 99).

Rabbinic teaching and understanding also follow in this spirit, mind, and body concept. According to Kaplan (2017), the "ancient Hebrew word for soul, *nefesh*, has been classically understood as enjoying an integrated relationship with the body – a true and cooperative synthesis between body and soul which aligns with leading edge neuropsychological and neuro-psychoanalytic research on the mind/body connection" (7-8). Kaplan points out that much of modern psychiatry instead depends on ancient Greek thinking. Kaplan suggests that most people fail to realize just how much the contemporary mental health establishment has unwittingly bought into the way of Athens instead of Jerusalem), saying, "Even the word *psyche* derives from the Greek word for soul and implies a dissociation with the *soma* (body)" (7). Biblical thought shows that our spirit and our body cannot be dissociated. Rabbinic and Talmudic teaching has emphasized this connection for centuries, but these lessons were regarded as "a purely religious code" and not integrated into any kind of systematic program or understanding (11). These biblical views are not new; they have just been pushed aside for the perspectives and norms of Greco-Roman culture. As this Judeo-Christian perspective continues to be re-examined, it gives voice to the idea that God has connected our aspects since the very time of creation.

The Hebrew term *tselem,* according to Scot McKnight (2007), means "image," as in the "image of God" derived from Genesis 1:26-27 (17). The Greek translation for this "image" is "Eikon" (18). As the ones designed to represent God in this world, we become "cracked" Eikons in Genesis 3 because of the Fall. We still bear the image of God, but that brokenness is evident in how we act and operate. The design of body, mind, and spirit is not altered, but our three-part being is impacted by our fallen nature.

Scripture and the church clearly emphasize our spiritual separation from God (Rom. 5:12; 6:23). Spiritual death resulted in our sin. But, what about the other aspects of our being? Were the mind and body affected by the Fall? Yes, all three aspects were. This is an important truth for the church to teach and share with disciples. If the spirit was impacted by the fall of man, then the other aspects also must have been altered. Stanford says, "Yet the church emphasizes the spiritual effects of sin while minimizing or disregarding the mental and physical effects" (Stanford, 2008, 12). He continues, "I think this results from a misunderstanding of what the scriptures teach about how we have been created" (12-13). I agree with Stanford's reasoning and assessment. The fall has impacted all three aspects of our being. We are all cracked image bearers of God.

There is nothing wrong with saying that our bodies are damaged because of sin. We age. We get sick. We suffer physically. The same can be said of our minds and mental health. Certain segments of the church seem to have developed a subtle Gnosticism as it relates to caring for people, due to a devaluation of the importance of people's physical, material selves. These Gnostic segments seem to treasure the spiritual but find the physical and mental aspects of our being as obstacles. There is no clear reason or way to identify why this persists within the American church, and the reasons vary widely. They may be cultural stigma, ignorance, wrong teaching, bad biblical interpretation, or a poor understanding of the creation story, all of which have led many to reject our physiological and psychological needs and honor only our spiritual health needs. Prayer is not the only choice on the menu for healing, after all.

The church should not be afraid or unsure of psychology or medicine. Just as we do not think it unspiritual to medically treat someone with cancer, treatment for depression and mental illness also should be allowed. Medical and therapeutic methods are perfectly acceptable options in seeking care. We should see no difference between the person taking a prescription for heart disease and a person talking to a counselor for anorexia. When we examine the physiological, psychological, and theological aspects of our being, it honors God and how we were created. Knowledge, medicine, therapy, and treatment from these disciplines can contribute to our overall wellbeing. It is vital that we accept and incorporate all three into a person's realm of care.

While theology and psychology have been pitted against each other in the past, they should be viewed as different disciplines that both contribute to suicide prevention. Karen Mason (2014) says, "Psychology as an empirical science can provide pastoral caregivers a great deal of information about suicide but cannot make pronouncements about what's morally objectionable about suicide, whereas theology can" (23). There is truth and knowledge in physiological and psychological disciplines. She continues, "Some readers might be concerned that discovery of truth outside the Bible is a criticism of the Bible. It is not.... The Bible is not diminished because as God's inspired revelation it provides us the meaning of what we observe in science" (24). We should value psychology for what it can do and how it can address our mental health.

Likewise, people should value theology for what is can do and how it can address our spiritual health. Each discipline is separate, unique, and necessary to the holistic well-being of our three-part lives. Mason (2014) makes this point by sharing, "To blame psychology that it doesn't do theology is like being disappointed that a hammer can't bake bread. And to throw that hammer away is a waste of a good tool" (25). Our physical, mental, and spiritual aspects each require care. These separate disciplines need to be accepted and integrated into our care routines in order for suicide to be adequately addressed.

CHAPTER 2
SUICIDE

The Magnitude of Suicide

The magnitude of suicide is alarming. It reaches across communities, cities, states, and nations. It is a universal issue with a legacy of loss and sadness. Ramsay (2004) says, "Suicide is one of the most underestimated community health problems in the world. More people are dying from suicide than in all of the armed conflicts around the world and about the same or more than those dying from traffic accidents" (7). In 2018, suicide was responsible for 48,344 deaths in the United States, which is one suicide every 10.9 minutes (Drapeau 2020, 1). Visualizing this quantity of deaths can be staggering if one understands that 48,344 deaths is like having a fully-loaded Boeing 777 airliner crash every Monday, Wednesday, and Friday of the week for an entire year. This amount of death and destruction is horrifying to imagine, but it is happening every year in our country. Suicide is a silent public health crisis. For a multitude of different reasons, it feels like people and communities are silent in regard to this deadly killer.

Suicide spans nearly all age groups, proving that any age is vulnerable. Suicide is the third leading cause of death for youth 10-14 years of age, the second leading cause of death among people 15-34 years of age, the fourth leading cause of death among people 35-44 years of age, the fifth leading cause among people ages 45-54, and the eighth leading cause among people 55-64 years of age (Centers for Disease Control and Prevention 2020). These statistics are tragic, but they represent only a portion of the entire problem. These numbers reflect completed suicides. Substantially more people are hospitalized or treated in ambulatory settings as a result of suicidal behavior than those who are fatally injured (Stone 2017, 8). For every person who dies by suicide, as many as 100 times more people injure themselves from nonfatal suicidal behaviors (Ramsay 2004). Ramsay confirms that "Four to five percent of all people attempt suicide in their lifetime; one in nine have seriously considered suicide" (7).

Understanding Suicide

People can address suicide with knowledge and care for those who need help. Knowing the signs of suicide is incredibly important, and it allows a community to provide help for those in pain. Ramsay (2004) points out that "A sudden, painful event may set off or hasten a decision to die by suicide, but it is unlikely to be the only cause. More typically, other contributing events and feelings have occurred over a prolonged period of time" (22). Suicide can be addressed where we live. With help, human beings are capable of withstanding almost any kind of loss, turmoil, or suffering.

Another item to highlight is that suicides are often telegraphed. "Most people communicate how they are reacting to or feeling about the events that are drawing them toward suicide. These communications – or invitations for others to offer help – come in the form of direct statements, physical signs, emotional reactions, or behavioral cues" (Ramsay 2004, 23). People with suicidal thoughts normally share that suicide might be under consideration. Those at risk normally give warnings, but communities too often miss the invitations and cries for help. Education is vital to addressing suicide. Ignorance of the warning signs of suicide can prove to be fatal.

Serious talk about suicide needs to be a part of this effort. Discussing suicide does not plant the idea in people's minds. In fact, the exact opposite is true. Talking about suicide does not create or increase risk. It reduces risk. Ramsay (2004) points out that "Open talk and genuine concern about someone's thoughts of suicide are a source of relief for them and are often the key elements in preventing the immediate danger of suicide. Avoidance leaves the person at risk feeling more alone and perhaps too anxious to risk asking someone else to help" (23). Our conversations can save a life. "Most suicidal people are unsure about dying right up to the point of acting. Part of them wants to die, but part of them wants to live. Very few are absolutely determined or completely decided about ending their life. Most people are looking for help to avoid suicide" (25). Noticing and talking with people during this time of ambiguity is vital. David Jobes (2006) echoes this with his three essential truisms on suicide:

Most suicidal people do not want an end to their biological existence; rather, they want an end to their psychological pain and suffering. Most suicidal people tell others (including mental professionals) that they are thinking about suicide as a compelling option for coping with their pain. Most suicidal people have psychological problems, social problems, and poor methods for coping with pain – all things that mental health professionals are usually well trained to tackle (7).

Talking about suicide helps to alleviate that pain and suffering. Psychological pain is real and can drive people toward suicide. Keefe (2018) uses the term *psychache* to describe intense, unbearable psychological pain. When left unresolved, psychache leads to suicide, suicidal thoughts, or suicidal behavior (9). It is intense pain, not an illness. Discussions about suicide can address the hidden pain that one feels. Serious talk and openness surrounding the topic is necessary. We cannot, ought not, avoid discussions about suicide. Doing so could be fatal. It is critically important that caring individuals ask about the thoughts and struggles of suicide one may have.

Risk Factors

Invitations are signs of distress that invite the help of others. They communicate that a person may have suicidal thoughts or may be close to suicidal behavior. LivingWorks, Inc. (2014) suggests that there are five invitation categories that caring people should explore: actions, physical changes, words expressed, feelings, and stressful events. Figure 3 shows each category and provides a list of potential warning signs or invitations that should be explored if they arise.

Figure 3.

Explore Invitations

Explore Invitations

ACTIONS
- Giving away possessions
- Withdrawal (family, friends, school, work)
- Loss of interest in sports and leisure
- Misuse of alcohol, drugs
- Impulsive/reckless behavior
- Self-mutilation
- Extreme behavior changes

PHYSICAL
- Lack of interest in appearance
- Change/loss in sex interest
- Disturbed sleep
- Change/loss of appetite, weight
- Physical health complaints

WORDS
"All of my problems will end soon."
"No one can do anything to help me now."
"Now I know what they were going through."
"I just can't take it any more."
"I am a burden to everyone."
"I can't do anything right."
"I just can't think straight anymore."

FEELINGS
- Desperate
- Angry
- Guilty
- Worthless
- Lonely
- Sad
- Hopeless
- Helpless

STRESSFUL EVENTS
with **FEELINGS OF LOSS**

(LivingWorks 2014, 7).

Hearing someone utter the phrase, "All of my problems will soon be over," should be viewed as an invitation to talk. It could be a harmless statement, or it could be a red flag. Exploring this invitation to talk is the right course of action. The person may have gotten a new job, purchased a lottery ticket, made plans to move into a new apartment, or spoken with a divorce attorney. On the other hand, the person may be contemplating suicide. We cannot ascertain what the statement means until we explore the invitation. The vagueness and veiled nature of such a statement is unknown until we make time to stop, care, and ask what was meant by it.

Invitations are often identified as warning signs and risk factors, such as characteristics, conditions, or influences that increase the likelihood of suicide. People need to be educated about and aware of these. Suicide prevention seeks to reduce and or mitigate the risks while increasing the factors that protect people from suicide. Risk factors include prior suicide attempt(s), abuse of alcohol and other drugs, history of depression or other mental illnesses, isolation, chronic pain, hopelessness, and access to lethal means (Stone 2017, 8).

A prominent factor associated with suicide is the presence of a mental health concern. In the National Comorbidity Survey, "A mental health disorder was present in 82 percent of people with suicidal thoughts, 94.5 percent of those who made a suicide plan, and 88.2 percent of those who had attempted suicide in the previous twelve months" (Mason 2014, 34). Major depression was listed as the most common disorder in the survey. In a separate study, Joiner (2009) lists the "big five" mental health disorders of concern for suicide risk as "borderline personality disorder (400 times higher suicide rate than the that of the general population), anorexia nervosa (which increases suicide risk 23 times), major depressive disorder (20 times more risk), bipolar disorder (15 times greater risk), and schizophrenia (8.5 times greater risk)" (21, 44).

Having more than one mental health problem increases the risk of suicide attempt by five times (Mason 2014). Mason also points out that "Fifty-one percent of people who attempt suicide have both a mental health problem and a substance abuse problem" (34). Substance abuse is a risk factor for all age groups because it lowers inhibitions and impairs judgment. Having a mental health problem is not the entire story of suicide. It is not a catch-all explanation, because mental illness is much more common than suicide. "An estimated 26.2 percent of Americans ages eighteen and older (one in four adults) suffer from a diagnosable mental disorder in a given year" (Stanford 2008, 4). Every suicide is unique and encompasses multiple factors over time.

Protective Factors

Protective factors are characteristics, conditions, or influences that decrease the likelihood of suicide. In epidemiology, they are the "flipside" or the mirror image of risk factors (Koenig 1998). Just as risk factors highlight a negative effect, protective factors show the protective or preventive effect. "The typical way to describe the effects of a protective factor are to state that it protects against or prevents morbidity. This implies that the force of this effect is somehow to 'hold back' the tide of pathogenesis" (39). "Protective factors can counter a specific risk factor or buffer against a number of risks associated with suicide" (Stone 2017, 9). They act as a dam holding back all of the stresses, strains, issues, and contributing factors that may push someone toward suicide. We all have dams holding us back from suicide. Some people have dams with the strength of concrete, while others may have only an earthen dam made of mud and sticks. Eventually, there will be a storm in life that threatens to break our protective dam. While cracks may form in a person's dam, they can be repaired and bolstered. It is important to reinforce and strengthen protective factors, or else the dam may break, causing a total loss. Protective factors include social support, close family relationships, the presence of an intimate partner, coping skills, community connectedness, a sense of purpose or meaning in life, faith / religion / spirituality, access to treatment, and restricted access to lethal means (9). These connections with family members, friends, neighbors, and religious organizations "serve as potent protective factors against the risk of developing patterns of suicidal thoughts and behaviors (e.g., Borowsky et al., 2001; Knox et al., 2003; Oyama et al., 2004)" (Kaplan 2017, 75).

The presence of religion and spirituality as protective factors should not be a surprise. While some may consider religion to be superficial or antiquated, religion was a cornerstone to the first treatise on suicide. French sociologist Emile Durkheim's 1897 work in *Suicide* captured how and why religions protect believers from suicide. He showed that "Religious groups provide rules for many areas of life, and that these rules have a preservation function for individuals." Additionally, he found that religious groups "provide support and integration. Durkheim argued that individuals who were isolated from social life, who were not active participants in families, religious groups, or other community organizations, were more prone to suicide as well" (Koenig 1998, 52). Durkheim was the first to examine and show religious groups as supportive, integrative communities that deter suicide. Some camps may share criticism on the methodological grounds he used from that era, but recent tests and studies confirm his theories with social network theory, giving consistent support on suicide rates in the United States and abroad (53). His original work on religion is clearly relevant to the field of mental health and suicide prevention today. Religion, spirituality, and faith continue to be seen and shown as protective factors that combat suicide (Mason 2014, 18).

CHAPTER 3
SCRIPTURE

People turn to the Bible because it has been a source of spiritual strength, comfort, and guidance for centuries. The Bible inspires faith and provides direction for daily living. Scripture offers a message of hope and promise for people of all ages. As life's seasons change, the Bible offers us words of assurance, encouragement, refreshment, and hope. It is a book that allows us to grow over a lifetime. Growth includes faith and our closeness with God. Christians usually speak of the Bible as the Word of God and understand that it expresses God's will for people.[4] As the Word of God, the Bible is considered an authoritative book. The Bible was written by people but inspired by God. It is holy, sacred, and true. Most Protestant churches consider the Bible to be the primary authority in matters of faith and life. Roman Catholic and Orthodox churches hold that the Bible and church tradition together are authoritative for faith and morals. Scripture is incorporated into Christian worship services because it is the divine message for all of humanity. Sermons, homilies, and messages are communicated to congregants because the Bible is the sacred standard for us to use for all matters that touch our life.

Scripture must be the starting place for Christians to discuss suicide, because the message of scripture gives shape and direction to our lives. It shares how we find relationship with God and with each other. Our faith must be both vertical and horizontal. Vertical faith is our linkage with God, and horizontal faith encompasses our relationship with others. Horizontal faith also encompasses our relationship with ourselves, since we are to love others as we love ourselves (Mark 12:28-31). We cannot and should not close our eyes to advances in medicine or science; to neglect these would be irresponsible and uncaring to those we love. At the same time, we must recognize that there are dimensions of life that transcend these categories and subjects of contemporary life. When people engage medicine and science to discuss the meaning and purpose of life, they find themselves asking inherently religious questions. They may not use the language of religion to do so, but Christians contend that all discussions about the meaning and purpose of life are inextricably bound up with God and matters related to God. It is only fitting that scripture be applied to this arena. The Bible is needed to evaluate and assess the context of suicide, because it is the God-given blueprint for life. If, as Christians contend, people exist in God's image (Gen. 1:27), then people cannot learn about themselves without also learning about God. The Bible is the correct starting place for Christians to discuss suicide. It is a vital resource from which to study life and apply our faith. The books of scripture are the spectacles that bring focus to our world and enable us to see with new eyes.

Why Suicide Is Wrong

Christianity is strongly against suicide. It carries a proscription on self-destruction due to the core beliefs of Christianity. God communicates through scripture and biblical principles that suicide is not his will for us. We are made in a unique fashion that demands preservation. God's Word declares the sanctity of life and demands that we preserve it. The Bible clearly shows us that suicide is the wrong choice. It establishes a moral code for us to follow, lays out divine instruction, and lists several examples of people dealing with suicidal circumstances. I will outline four core beliefs that Christians have and use to reject suicide.

The Image of God

First, people are made in the image of God. Suicide disregards the image of God within humanity. Nevertheless, as such, human life is inherently valuable. There is a transcendent human dignity in each of us. Every person, every life, has value. People are precious and should not be seen as anything less. In Genesis 1, God announces his crowning work to the heavenly host: "Let Us make man in Our image, according to Our likeness" (Gen. 1:26-27). Once human beings enter the creation story, we become God's earthly representative and the focal point of God's kingdom. Since humanity is made in God's image, every human being is worthy of love, honor, and respect. While God values all of creation, we are set apart from the rest of creation, due to his unique will for us. We carry part of our Creator in us and are called to reflect our divine nature on Earth.

David Closson laments our fall from this image but rejoices in our redemption in Christ:

> One of the tragic results of sin is that man no longer properly images God; the remnants of the image have been marred. The relationship with our Creator is broken, and redemptive history bears witness to man's inability to obey and honor God. But the glorious truth of the New Testament is that restoration is possible through Christ, the perfect image of God (Col. 1:15), whose redeeming work restores the image to repentant sinners and establishes them as co-heirs with Christ. (2016)

Our image, while once distorted from the fall, can be restored and made right through Jesus. Our new characteristics can again reflect the brightness of God in "righteousness and holiness" (Eph. 4:24). Believers are called to be "conformed to the image" of Christ and will someday be "like Him" (Rom. 8:29; 1 John 3:2). It is right and proper for us to look into the faces of people and imagine seeing Jesus.

Suicide is Self-Murder

Second, suicide is a violation of the sixth commandment, "You shall not murder" (Exod. 20:13; Deut. 5:17). Murder is clearly identified as a sin. Murder is the taking of life without legal or moral justification.[5] There are many Hebrew and Greek words for *kill*, but the term used in the commandment specifically says murder. The Hebrew for this verb usually refers to a premeditated and deliberate act wherein one is slaughtered or dashed to pieces (Strong 1996, 134). Just as Cain slew his brother, there is an intent to end someone's life. Taking life in this manner is against God's law. A. A. Howsepian, writes, "All murders are, after all, wrongful killings of certain sorts, namely, those wrongful killings that are constituted by one's intentionally bringing about the deaths of innocent persons" (1998, 300). The Bible is not mute on suicide. Terminating life goes against the way of God. He speaks strongly on the matter:

> It is immediately apparent from the OT that murder is unspeakably abhorrent for at least two reasons: (1) It is the irremedial and permanent destruction of life, the most precious possession an individual can ever have; (2) It is an assault upon God Himself, for every human being without exception is an image-bearer of his Creator.... There is not only inherent value in humanity – there is imputed value as well. (324)

Murder contradicts the priceless worth that God has placed on every human being. Suicide is a subset of this commandment. It is ending your own life, or self-murder, as the Latin root of the word suggests.

The purpose of the law was first to show us God's perfect standard and the unchanging nature of God. It emphasizes prohibition. The law also emphasizes our vertical and horizontal relationships. The law should be followed out of respect for God and out of respect for humankind. Christians will also emphasize that our obedience to the law is not just legal but out of love for Jesus. We wish to follow all of the commandments out of love toward others as well as toward ourselves. God wants us to live beyond mere behavior and acts. God wants to create the kind of heart that generates good, righteous, and holy behavior. God does not merely want people to obey rules for the sake of obedience. God wants us to be holy as God is holy and to value what he values. Murder clearly goes against the values of God, and suicide falls into the same category. Since each life is precious and treasured by the Almighty, we should not practice suicide.

The prohibition against murder is so important that it is given to Noah and his family immediately after the flood. This likely predates the Exodus account by more than 1,000 years.[6] Here, God reminds humanity that we are made in his image and are valuable in his sight, and we are to honor the sanctity of human life. God's high regard for life means that murder will not be tolerated. The covenant with Noah emphasizes a new beginning and a divine promise never to destroy earthly life with a flood. Part of this new beginning points back to the Garden and reminds people of their own worth: "Whoever sheds man's blood, by man his blood shall be shed, for in the image of God He made man"

(Gen. 9:6).[7] Some may look at this verse and say that it is cold and uncaring or that it institutes capital punishment on the Earth. God gives this edict as a way to save and preserve life, not to take it. We are precious and valued in the sight of God. There is no other person on Earth with my genetic code or thumbprint. We are all unique and beyond price. Life has absolute value, and if it is violated with spilt blood, then there is a penalty for violating its sanctity. A murderer demonstrates contempt for God and for all of humanity, not for just their victim. Spilling blood is the wrong action and goes against the new beginning God provided to Noah and his descendants. Ending your own life by suicide is a category of murder. It is self-murder. Scripture defines murder as the premeditated destruction of life; therefore, suicide as a premeditated self-killing is a category of murder (Demy 1998, 315-316).[8]

Our Lives Belong to God

Third, God is the owner and giver of life. We are not our own but stewards of a life that God has given. Life is a precious gift, and it is not to be thrown away or abandoned. If God is the Lord of all that is, then he retains ownership over our lives and all of our days. God is the only one who can determine when our service is complete and our intended purpose fulfilled. Suicide can be viewed as the chief example of self-idolatry. Since we belong to God, then life is not something to be thrown away. We should view life as sacred and precious. Scripture is clear and consistent in teaching that our lives belong to our Creator and that we are not to end life for our own purposes, no matter how distraught or hopeless we might feel. This life belongs to God. In good times and in difficulty, we are called to honor God with our life.

Job had several catastrophes befall him and his family. Hearing the news of these personal atrocities, Job utters, "Naked I came from my mother's womb, and naked I shall return there. The Lord gave and the Lord has taken away. Blessed be the name of the Lord" (Job 1:21). In all of the heart-wrenching hurt and drama, Job did not sin or blame God (Job 1:22). He is deeply grieved and wrestles with suicide by strangling (Job 7:15). However, Job does not act on this. As the story proceeds, "Job reaffirms his relationship with his Creator: 'Though He slay me, yet will I trust in Him' (Job 13:15)" (Kaplan 2017, 111).

Job was able to argue within the relationship he had with God without leaving it. It is important to amplify this point of scripture. He understood that his life did not belong to him but to God. God breathes life into us (Gen. 2:7), and it is God who takes it away (Job 34:13-15). The example of Job is powerful and instructive. As he did, we also can choose to keep living.

The story of Job is about the goodness of God even in the midst of human suffering and calamity. We do not earn merit with good works, nor do we lose favor from a lack of obedience. God cannot be reduced to a transactional relationship, like putting coins into a vending machine. God does not award points based on our good behavior. A simple reading of Job elicits the humanity of the story. A deeper reading plumbs the theological richness of God's sovereignty and prerogative in life and death. This is shown especially in the conversations between Job and his friends. Despite the trials and tribulations of Job, he refused to take his own life.

No one is exempt from human suffering, but we are all called to remain and continue as faithful servants, no matter the current trials. We do not belong to ourselves. Our lives are in the hands of God, who has a plan, a purpose, and a reason for us to exist, even if at times we forget these truths.

Paul writes to the Corinthian church and reminds them that the body belongs to the Lord. While some may feel they have a right to do anything they please, Paul argues that total freedom of action may not benefit the believer. What we do with our physical body is important, because God has regard for our earthly vessel. Paul reminds the church that a body destined for resurrection should not be used for immorality (1 Cor. 6:14). It is not merely the spirit that is a member of Christ but the whole person, consisting of spirit and physical body. Since the body is so precious to God, nothing should be done to harm it. There are immoral actions outside the body and internally; nevertheless, the body is a sacred place where God dwells. Paul asks, "Or do you not know that your body is a temple of the Holy Spirit who is in you, whom you have from God, and that you are not your own? For you have been bought with a price: therefore, glorify God in your body" (1 Cor. 6:19-20).[9] Paul is concerned with more than the use and misuse of our body. He is concerned with how we relate to God. Do we follow from fear of punishment or from the closeness of our heart?

Suicide Harms Community

Fourth, suicide cannot be justified because it harms the entire community where we live. Suicide hurts a multitude of people, not just one individual. It injures those around us and even far beyond. Hauerwas writes that "One should not commit suicide because of one's duty to others in the community. People should not be viewed as atomistic individuals who are unconnected to others" (Hauerwas 1998, 190). This addresses our horizontal relationship of faith. We are called to love and care for those around us. In Mark's gospel, Jesus is asked to name the most important or the greatest commandment. He gives two responses, "And you shall love the Lord your God with all your heart, and with all your soul, and with all your mind, and with all your strength. The second is this, you shall love your neighbor as yourself. There is no commandment greater than these" (Mark 12:30-31). Jesus pointed to Deuteronomy 6:4-5 and Leviticus 19:18, two very important passages. Jesus combined the two Old Testament passages to show that the love for our neighbor is a natural outgrowth of our love for God. The horizontal and vertical are deeply connected. Typically, when we hear the second commandment, people reflect on the need to think more highly of others because of a great love of self. Our pride, self-confidence, and inflated egos have gotten in the way of loving others; we overly prize ourselves. Of course, such narcissistic characteristics are contrary to loving others, as we are to love ourselves as well as them. But, the opposite is also true in this passage. Our sorrow, despair, despondence, and depression can show how little we love ourselves. We can have a self-attitude that is too small. The commandment shows that we must properly love self and then share that love with our neighbor. Again, Jesus shows us the importance of connecting the love of God and the love of neighbor. It means loving myself and also sharing that love with the entire community.

The community is large and complex and has many parts. While community is often touted in the routine categories of family, friends, and neighbors, scripture calls us to love people outside of these comfortable and familiar circles. We are called to also love difficult people, not just those we treasure. We are even called upon to love our enemies and pray for those who persecute us (Matt. 5:44). The community is much larger than we often imagine. Paul points out, "There is one body, but it has many parts" (1 Cor. 12:12). A hand is different from a foot. An ear is different from an eye. One part of the body cannot be any less because it is different. These different parts are necessary for the entire body. The whole body cannot be an eye. It is necessary for the entire body parts to function together. Many parts, pieces, and members are required for the body to work. God has placed the members together in the body, just as He desired. It is not our place to call one out and say that there is no need for a particular part. Instead, there should be no division in the body, and the members should "have the same care for one another" (1 Cor. 12:25). The community needs each part in the body, each person that God has given. Suicide injures more than the individual; it harms the entire community. Suicide leaves an enormous hole in homes, families, congregations, and our society that was never intended. God's blueprint would avoid this injury, pain, and suffering for communities.

These four biblical principles and concepts have resulted in a longstanding Judeo-Christian belief that suicide is wrong. While some may point to the Bible and proclaim that there is no clear scriptural prohibition against self-destruction, Christian interpretation shows that suicide is contrary to the heart of God. We are called to see value in others and share the love of God as a lifestyle that demonstrates the kingdom of God.

Suicidal Thoughts and Attempts

Suicide, depression, and suicidal thoughts are not sugar-coated in scripture. In fact, they are even seen in some of God's prophets and ministers. Even the most mature believers are susceptible to depression and suicidal thoughts. Several of the people whom we lift up as saints and pillars of faith were at the end of their rope, physically exhausted, or disillusioned. Prophets and ministers became so frustrated with their ministry that they asked God to kill them or cursed the day of their birth. Examples and times of hopelessness can be seen in Moses, Job, Elijah, Jonah, and Jeremiah (Num. 11:12-15, Job 3:1-3, 1 Kings 19:4, Jonah 4:1-11, Jer. 20:14-18). They asked God to take their lives, but in every case, God refused. Scripture also records women who thought about killing themselves and instead chose life: Rebekah (Gen. 27:46) and Rachel (Gen. 30:1). These two women utter the first suicidal statements found in scripture, but they are steadfast and continue on in life. The Bible has several accounts of potential tragedies that do not end in disaster. It is important for us to share these stories from scripture. They remind us that the hope we find in God is far greater than what we find in the world.

David was the most revered king of Israel. Scripture describes him as a man after God's own heart (vis-à-vis, Saul), but even he struggled with times of depression. The Psalms record many examples of despair, despondency, and pleas for deliverance. A few of these examples are in Psalms: 22, 32, 35, 38, 40, 42, 51, 52, 54-57, 59, 63, and 69. As a warrior, David endured trials and suffering with long campaigns of people seeking to end his life. He was forced to flee Jerusalem, hide in caves, and move around the rugged countryside of Israel to escape the wrath of his own father-in-law. David was separated from family and friends. He endured incredible stress and torment as a man on the run. As a fallen man, he felt separated and distant from God. After being confronted by the prophet Nathan, David suffered with great emotional anguish over his affair with Bathsheba, the murder of Uriah the Hittite, and the aftermath of these poor choices. He wrote as many as three psalms expressing his grief and anguish during those dark days of his life. It does not matter in what stage of life we read his writings, the Psalms clearly show us a window into the inner turmoil he felt and endured.

John the Baptist is proclaimed in scripture as a great and holy man. He was greater than earlier prophets were because he proclaimed a fuller message of coming salvation (Matt. 11:10, 13:17). God sent John to prepare the way for Jesus and call Israel to repentance. John was a wilderness prophet and was the first one to declare Jesus' identity as the Messiah. John proclaims that Jesus would baptize with fire, establish a new kingdom, and bring judgment upon the Earth. His call is the same message of Jesus: "Repent, for the kingdom of heaven is near" (Matt. 3:2, 4:17). But, in prison, it seemed that John the Baptist was struggling with misunderstanding, discouragement, despair, and doubt. John sent some of his followers to question Jesus about his eschatological promises

(Matt. 11:2-3). John's expectations about the Messiah's future role were correct, but John did not understand that Jesus had another mission before the coming judgment. Being in prison likely meant John's time was short, and he expected to see this great coming of the Lord. God does not always act as we expect, nor does God always operate on the timeline we think is best. Jesus encourages a broken man of God by telling John's disciples that "The blind receive their sight, and the lame walk, the lepers are cleansed and the deaf hear, the dead are raised up, and the poor have the gospel preached to them" (Matt. 11:5). Jesus said this so that John could hear his message and be encouraged with the reminder of Isaiah's description of the messianic era. While John struggled with common weaknesses like doubt, we can draw encouragement from these trials. God uses imperfect people even while he is calling us to greater maturity through him.

Even the most mature believers are susceptible to depression. Those closest to Jesus are not immune from feelings of despair. Peter, the first disciple to declare Jesus as the Messiah, denies Jesus three times as he sat in the courtyard of the high priest. Each time, Peter's words become more enflamed. During the second denial, he used an oath proclaiming he did not know Jesus. In the third statement, Peter began to curse and swear prior to his denial. After Peter heard the rooster crow, he remembered the foretelling words of Jesus and was terribly distraught by what he had done. Scripture records that Peter ran out and wept bitterly (Matt. 26:69-75). In this moment of crisis, we can easily imagine Peter as a broken man. Moments earlier in the Garden of Gethsemane, Peter was prepared to wield a sword against the Roman cohort and temple guards (John 18:3) and likely die trying to kill or subdue those who would capture Jesus. Now, he is willing to renounce his faith and deny Jesus, the Lord he had promised to never deny (Matt. 10:33; 26:35). How should he respond to this failure of discipleship? Peter shows us that the best response to failure is repentance, not sorrow unto death like Judas. We see that anyone can start again after a failure, no matter the size and scope of the wrong committed.

The apostle Paul made comments about an internal conflict of wishing to die and be present with the Lord or carrying on while in prison (Phil. 1:19-26). He also spoke of an affliction that came to him and Timothy in Asia. They were so burdened beyond their own strength that they despaired even of life (2 Cor. 1:8-10). We also find stories like the Philippian jailer who drew his sword and was about to kill himself because he thought Paul and Silas had escaped their prison cell. The suicide attempt was quickly thwarted when Paul cried out, "Do not harm yourself, for we are all here" (Acts 16:28). This biblical example shows how quickly an acute moment of crisis can turn anyone to suicidal behavior when hope is lost. The story makes a dramatic turn as the Philippian jailer seeks to know the peace and comfort of faith in Christ and, that night, places his faith and hope in Jesus. Scripture records that the jailer and all his household were later baptized (Acts 16:31-34).

Throughout the Bible are clear examples of men and women who thought about ending their lives and chose not to; we should follow their example. In all of these potentially life and death situations, people were tempted to consider ending it all, but instead chose life. No matter how bad a situation may seem, we can turn to God in our sorrow and our shame. These instances provide biblical evidence that suicide is never the right choice to make. It also shows that God is always present and ready to hear our cry. Christians are called to remain steadfast in the midst of trials (2 Cor. 12:7-10; Phil. 4:11-13; James 1:2-4). The entire story of scripture is redemption and restoration for those who will confess and turn back to a loving, gracious God.

Leland Ryken (1998) has written extensively on the literary nature of the Bible from an evangelical perspective:

> In most of these stories the tragedy is averted through the protagonist's repentance and God's forgiveness. The story of David's repentance after his sin with Bathsheba and Uriah is the great paradigm. The world of literary tragedy is usually a closed world. Once the hero has made the tragic choice, there is no escape. But the Bible is preoccupied with what is more than tragic – with the redemptive potential in human tragedy. In the stories of the Bible, there is always a way out, even after the tragic mistake has been made. (362)

Scripture shows that we can commit to obey God and respect human life, including our own. The Bible declares that God's people should choose life over death (Deut. 30:15, 19). Even in the midst of bad choices and wrong actions, God wants us to make a giant U-turn and come back to his tender care. No one is too far from God. We can all return and be welcomed back, because the good news of Jesus still applies today. We are never cast away from the loving care of Christ and are direct beneficiaries of His atoning work on the cross. We can choose life and bask in the warmth of God's eternal love.

Examples of Suicide

God's word does not use the term suicide anywhere in scripture, but it has much to say on the subject. Scripture provides six accounts of suicide in the Old Testament, and one in the New Testament. The suicide accounts are Abimelech in Judges 9:54, Samson in Judges 16:29-30, Saul in 1 Samuel 31:4, Saul's armor bearer in 1 Samuel 31:5, Ahithophel in 2 Samuel 17:23, Zimri in 1 Kings 16:18, and Judas in Matthew 27:5. Of these, the death of Abimelech could initially be called an "assisted" suicide. Some also want to describe Samson's death as a type of "martyrdom" or categorize it as the heroic loss of a soldier (Brand et al. 2003, 1540). Regardless of classification, the Bible presents each person who dies by suicide as an individual whose behavior should not be emulated. I will examine all seven suicide accounts and refrain from classifying them as anything other than a suicide.

Abimelech

Abimelech started a campaign to become king after his father Gideon died. Instead of using prayer or seeking God's path, he used deceit, violence, and murder as methods to secure a place of power over God's people. He carved out a principality for himself by means of brutality and force. Scripture records he went to Gideon's house at Ophrah and murdered seventy of his brothers on one stone (Judg. 9:5). If people started to question his methods, he would burn their city and kill all the inhabitants. Abimelech even killed his mother's relatives and fellow tribesmen in Shechem. These were the very people who set him up to become king and financed his efforts with seventy pieces of silver (Judg. 9:4). Scripture records that he set the tower of Shechem on fire killing one thousand men and women (Judg. 9:49). During another campaign, Abimelech took the city and was preparing to set a tower on fire. As he drew near the door of the tower, a woman threw a millstone upon Abimelech's head and crushed his skull. Already having a mortal wound, he called for his armor bearer and pleaded, "Draw your sword and kill me, so that it will not be said of me, 'A woman slew him'" (Judg. 9:54). Abimelech considered it more "manly" to be killed by his own armor bearer. His final act of hubris reflected the poor decisions and consequences surrounding his life. Scripture records that "God repaid the wickedness of Abimelech, which he had done to his father in killing his seventy brothers" (Judg. 9:56).

Samson

Samson might be the most well-known suicide in the Old Testament. It is also a terribly sad and complex story. After a life dedicated to fighting Philistines, Samson lost his strength, was captured, and spent his last years blinded and tormented by his enemies. As the Philistines were celebrating and sacrificing to their deity Dagon for the triumph over Samson and the God of Israel, he was released from prison to amuse the crowd. A small child leads Samson to the temple. This was likely considered an insult and a showing of Philistine strength, as Walton (2000) explains: "The entertainment provided by Samson was probably not connected to his wit or his strength, but to his blindness. Putting obstacles in the way and striking or tripping him would be only a few of the cruel possibilities for tormenting a blind person in an unfamiliar place" (270). In a final act, Samson prayed for his strength to return and "to be avenged of the Philistines for my two eyes" (Judg. 16:28). Samson grabs the support pillars bracing the entire structure and causes it to collapse. The temple is destroyed and over 3,000 Philistines perish. "The episode ends by crediting Samson with having killed more Philistines at his death than in all his life before. His family then came and buried him in his father's tomb. Great respect for Samson continued through the centuries and his name was included among those 'heroes of faith' listed by the author of the Epistle to the Hebrews" (Clemons 1990, 21). His suicide is often considered a heroic death. The Philistines were at war with the Israelites during this time and Samson sought to defeat Israel's enemy. When Samson literally brings the house down, he is again attempting to accomplish his mission of freeing Israel from the Philistines. Kaplan (2017) highlights this point in writing, "Significantly, his final action in life leads to a long period of peace (Judges 13)" (66). This death by choice example is frequently termed the supreme sacrifice among today's armed forces. We would compare it to a soldier jumping on a grenade to save his squad. Others argue that Samson did not take his life; he sacrificed his life. This camp wants to make a distinction between suicide and the willful self-sacrifice of one's own life. Instead of calling it a suicide, some call this a sacrificial death or an indirect suicide. They dispute Samson's death being a suicide, because they view it as an example of divinely-enabled self-sacrifice after repentance. Rachel Harris (2012) outlines that "Samson was often considered a Christ-like figure dying for the sins of others. Within Jewish culture, there was a greater focus on interpreting Samson's story as a parable of man's weakness and his need to repent. Samson's suicide was understood as an individual's sacrifice for his people" (70).

Saul and Saul's Armor Bearer

Saul, the first King of Israel, ended his life by suicide. His life came to its sad end in a battle in which three of his sons were killed, his army was routed, and he was badly wounded. Clemons (1990) points out that "He faced the certainty of capture, ridicule, and torture by his enemies" (16). Saul did not face good prospects if captured alive. In this period, it was common for kings to be mutilated and subjected to a life of humiliation. The Book of Judges states how putting out the eyes or cutting off the thumbs and big toes of enemies were just a few of the procedures used (Judg. 1:6-7; 16:21). "As a sign of their ignominy, they were doomed to spend miserable years begging and fighting for scraps under the triumphant king's table or displayed in public places for whatever abuse passersby might invent" (Walton 2000, 321). Saul said to his armor bearer, "Draw your sword and run me through, or these uncircumcised fellows will come and run me through and make sport of me. But the armor bearer would not; for he feared greatly. Therefore, Saul took his own sword and fell on it" (1 Sam. 31:4). When the armor bearer saw that Saul was dead, he fell on his own sword and died with him. Samuel shares this story as a narrative piece of literature. This type of writing focuses on the facts of the matter. He does not editorialize. The moral and ethical application of Saul's decision does not need to be addressed. It is already present. Later, Samuel emphasized the tragedy of this loss.

Samuel underscores this tragedy and the continuing grief of the community in the first chapter of 2 Samuel. Scripture records David weeping, mourning, and fasting when he hears the news of the loss. It also contains a psalm of lament over the death of Saul and Jonathan. No direct stigma or disgrace is placed on the manner of death, only sadness due to the unfortunate loss of Saul, his sons, and the people of Israel. Later, when David heard about the valiant men of Jabesh Gilead burying and honoring Saul, he asked for the Lord's blessing on them. We should allow this point of scripture to soak in a little bit. Those who honored and revered Saul, a man who died by his own hand, were in turn honored by David. Clemons (1990) believes that "The biblical writer further shaped the idea in the minds of the Israelites that no condemnation was to be heaped upon those who treated suicides with respect" (18).

Ahithophel

Ahithophel the Gilonite was a chief counselor and adviser to King David. He was likely considered essential for operating the kingdom. His advice "was like that of one who inquires of God. That was how both David and Absalom regarded all of Ahithophel's advice" (2 Sam. 16:23). Ahithophel joined Absalom's rebellion against King David. He offered a plan to defeat David, but Absalom did not follow it. After his counsel to the would-be king Absalom had been rejected, Ahithophel left the camp. Scripture does not record if he was upset for being second-guessed by others in the inner circle, ashamed for losing influence, or disgusted that he could not convince Absalom of how to proceed against his father. Ahithophel may have even surmised that Absalom's revolt would soon fail with this foolhardy plan, assuring David victory. If so, then David would return as king and likely deal with his betrayal. Ahithophel now faced a moment of crisis: the loss of credibility under Absalom or the potential loss of life under David. Rabbinic writers have also argued that "Since Ahithophel dies by suicide, his family inherits his estate. If he were to be executed as a rebel, his possessions would be forfeited to the king" (Kaplan 2017, 64). The Bible states that he saddled his donkey, went home, "set his house in order," and hanged himself. He died and was buried in his father's tomb.

Zimri

Zimri was the fifth king of the northern kingdom of Israel. His reign was the shortest of all the kings of Israel – only seven days. Scripture introduces Zimri as a chariot captain who usurped the throne by murdering his master King Elah. His treachery and timing are emphasized in scripture because he waited until Elah was drunk to kill him. He also waited to assassinate the King until the Israelite army was gone, fighting against Philistine Gibbethon. This gave Zimri time to claim the crown and move quickly to protect his hold on the throne. He killed the entire household of King Baasha, Elah's father, and all the male heirs of Elah. When members of the army had learned of what Zimri had done, they appointed Omri as their commander and withdrew to attack Tirzah, the royal city. "When Zimri saw that the city was taken, he went into the citadel of the king's house, and burned the king's house over him with fire, and died" (1 Kings 16:18-19). Much like Saul, Zimri was afraid to fall into the hands of his opponents. "Unlike Saul, however, his suicide most certainly resulted in the death of others for the palace was a public building in which others, too, must have sought refuge" (Merrill 1998, 323-324). This suicide multiplies the pain and suffering of Zimri's tragic act because it carries "the physical destruction of unwitting participants" (324). Scripture records that Zimri died because of the sins he had committed, doing evil in the sight of the Lord, walking in the way of Jeroboam (1 Kings 16:19). His name later became a byword for king killers and unfaithful servants (2 Kings 9:31).

Judas

Judas Iscariot is the last suicide mentioned in the Bible. He was one of the twelve disciples of Jesus and the only one from Judea. "All of the Gospels place him at the end of the list of disciples because of his role as a betrayer" (Brand et al. 2003, 959). John 12:4-6 records that Judas acted as treasurer for the group but was known as a miser and a thief. Matthew 27 gives us the only direct account of suicide in the New Testament. Of the four gospels, only Matthew makes reference to how Judas dies:

Then when Judas, who had betrayed Him, saw that He had been condemned, he felt remorse and returned the thirty pieces of silver to the chief priests and elders, saying, "I have sinned by betraying innocent blood." However, they said, "What is that to us? See to that yourself!" And he threw the thirty pieces of silver into the temple sanctuary and departed, and he went away and hanged himself (Matt. 27:3-5).

Another account of Judas's death occurs in the Book of Acts, where there is no indication that it was a suicide or that it was a result of betraying Jesus. In the Matthew account, Judas showed remorse, looked for the Pharisees, and returned the money. In his despair, Judas returned to his default position – focused on money. While money had given him happiness in the past, the returned purse did not provide peace. In fact, money gave him no comfort or solace at all. Unfortunately, in his time of sorrow, he never looked for God and did not return with a repentant heart. Nor does scripture record Judas seeking out a friend, companion, or brother to support him. Judas was not the only betrayer of Jesus that night. Simon Peter also felt remorse for denying Jesus three times but later found comfort with friends and returned with penitence. This is a stark contrast to the tragic choice of Judas. I believe that Judas is the saddest suicide story in the Bible. Judas journeyed with Jesus for three years, heard his teachings, and witnessed miraculous acts. It is hard to imagine that in all of his despair and despondency, Judas would not think of turning to God for forgiveness, love, and hope. Instead, his story ends with sorrow, never looking for God. However, to be honest, this is the tragic story of every suicide. One turns toward despair, forsakes the help and support of the community around them, and avoids God to the point of destruction. There was a turning point, but it was not taken.

Looking at these seven stories, one truth quickly arises: they did not have to end this way. They could have chosen a different path. Most of their stories reflect a variety of bad personal choices and unrepentant lives that could have been redeemed with the love of God. Yes, these individuals were dubious characters, but they were not beyond the mercy of God. Scripture records that none of them is personally praised for his actions. It is also safe to say that these men went through a period of spiritual collapse before they ended their own lives by suicide. Many of the biblical examples were in pain and afraid. Shame, regret, and despair loom large in their story. Their suffering, pain, and anguish, even though it happened in antiquity, is no different from the suffering that anyone can experience today. Suffering can be physical, mental, or spiritual. Christianity acknowledges the emptiness and brokenness that people feel, yet, it does not encourage suicide, because that choice communicates that there is no answer for despair. This is the opposite of the gospel message that scripture promises.

Was the Death of Jesus a Suicide?

Some suggest that the death of Jesus was a suicide. These arguments are mainly from those who interpret Jesus to be purely a human teacher. These ideas can also arise from those who deny the deity of Jesus or those who have little to no knowledge of Christianity. I suggest that the death of Jesus is not a suicide for three simple reasons.

Jesus Did Not Kill Himself

First, Jesus did not take his own life. He did not perform the destructive act of suicide or self-murder. While crucifixion is a violent and horrible death, Jesus did not kill himself. He did not place himself on the cross or drive nails into his own body. His death sentence was not self-imposed or self-inflicted. These things were done to him, not by him.

Some try to categorize the death of Jesus as an assisted suicide. This point of view argues that Jesus makes blasphemous and treasonous statements to end his life, tailors his religious movement so that governmental authorities will take his life, or remains silent in multiple court settings to guarantee his own death. This assisted suicide category is one wherein "An individual wants to die in the near term as the result of human intervention but not directly by his own hand" (Cooley 2020, 2). Such a death can be likened to a person pointing an empty gun at a law enforcement officer, hoping to die from the act. The officer sees the weapon and responds by using lethal force to subdue the assailant. There is no way for the officer to tell if the gun is loaded or empty, forcing him or her to respond or potentially die. Only later does one learn that the assailant had no intention of killing the officer. The assailant wanted to end his or her own life. Some argue that this "death by cop" approach would allow Jesus to die a self-embraced death and be viewed as a martyr (Cooley 2020, 2 and Mazrui 1965, 10). Suggesting that the crucifixion of Jesus is a suicide or a martyr's death frankly denies the beliefs and theology of Christianity. It would still require Jesus to participate in the act of suicide, suggesting that he can fall or sin. This would mean that the last Adam is equal to the first.

Jesus Does Not Sin

Second, scripture states that Jesus never sinned (2 Cor. 5:21, Heb. 4:15, Heb. 7:26, 1 Pet. 2:22). He knew no sin. Jesus was unstained by sin; hence, he is viewed as the perfect and unblemished Lamb of God. There are two theological positions that divide on the issue of Jesus being able to sin; the impeccability and the peccability of Jesus. Impeccability argues that it is impossible for Jesus to sin and to yield to temptation, because God cannot sin. Peccability argues that Jesus experienced temptation and was able to sin, but never did so. One can be in either camp and still agree with the scriptural accounts that Jesus did not sin and does not sin. The impeccability camp represents the majority of Christianity. Breaking the sixth commandment would constitute a breach of fellowship with God. Jesus cannot take a position or action against God because he obeys the Father in all things. The two are one. They are in union with each other, preventing Jesus from abandoning God's will. If Jesus sins, then it means that God sins. The death of Jesus cannot be a suicide because Jesus is one with the Father and carries out his will.

Jesus Has Two Natures

Third, the death of Jesus is not a suicide because Jesus exists with two natures. He is both divine and human. His death is not a suicide, nor is he a human martyr. Jesus exists as both God and man. His dual natures are a core belief of Christianity. This is explained in the Bible, the Nicene Creed in 325 AD, and the Chalcedonian Statement in 451 AD. The Chalcedonian understanding of how the divine and human aspects relate in Jesus Christ is that the humanity and divinity are exemplified as two natures and that there is a hypostatic union where the *Logos* perfectly subsists in these two natures. The Chalcedonian Statement affirms and insists on the unity of divine and human natures in Jesus. The First Council of Nicaea met to address the controversy of Arianism, an idea that Jesus was not divine but was, instead, a created being. The creed states that the Son is *homoousion tō Patri* (of one being with the Father), thus declaring Jesus to be completely divine. The Nicene Creed reads as follows:

We believe in one God,

the Father, the Almighty,

maker of heaven and earth,

of all that is, seen and unseen.

We believe in one Lord, Jesus Christ,

the only Son of God,

eternally begotten of the Father,

God from God, Light from Light,

true God from true God,

begotten, not made,

of one Being with the Father.

Through him all things were made.

For us and for our salvation he came down from heaven

by the power of the Holy Spirit

He became incarnate from the Virgin Mary,

and was made man.

For our sake he was crucified under Pontius Pilate;

he suffered death and was buried.

On the third day he rose again

in accordance with the Scriptures;

he ascended into heaven

and is seated at the right hand of the Father.

He will come again in glory to judge the living and the dead,

and his kingdom will have no end.

We believe in the Holy Spirit, the Lord, the giver of life,

who proceeds from the Father and the Son.

With the Father and the Son he is worshiped and glorified.

He has spoken through the Prophets.

We believe in one holy catholic and apostolic Church.

We acknowledge one baptism for the forgiveness of sins.

We look for the resurrection of the dead,

And the life of the world to come. Amen.

(Book of Common Prayer, 358-359)

Jesus had a human nature and physical body. Jesus also has a divine nature. This nature cannot be killed with metal nails, a soldier's spear, or a wooden cross. The Logos who existed with God prior to the sun, moon, and stars being set in the sky is deity and simply cannot be killed by human hands. A human being cannot kill Jesus Christ. Jesus is transcendent. He exists beyond human physical form and surpasses our limited human nature. That being said, Jesus became incarnate and yielded his place in Heaven for our sake. Incarnate simply means that Jesus took human form. The physical body that Mary delivered by birth in

Bethlehem does die in the crucifixion. Jesus dies a physical death on the cross and voluntarily surrenders his spirit to God the Father.

Luke 23:46 records, "And Jesus, crying out with a loud voice, said, 'Father, into Your hands I commit My spirit.' Having said this, He breathed His last." Here, Jesus recites Psalm 31:5, a verse used as a daily prayer given each evening. It communicates total trust in God and bright hope for a new day. As Jesus lets go of life, he knows that he can entrust God with the future. These words are not full of pain, darkness, or despair, as we would expect from one with suicidal thoughts, but rather with the firm knowledge of a compassionate Lord. Jesus has not given up on the world or this life as a suicidal individual resigned to defeat. He does not believe that humanity is a lost cause. He, instead, wants us to know that life and love are available in God the Father.

Luke, the consummate physician, was careful to specify the point of Jesus dying on the cross. His breathing stopped because He was dead. His spirit and his body were no longer joined. The word for spirit is "*pneuma*," or breath of life. This refers to the personal spirit of Jesus, one aspect of his human self. Jesus allowed himself – or his physical body – to die so that we may live and know eternal life. This is the promise and fulfillment of scripture.

Jesus dies on the cross as the "Lamb of God" who came to take away the sins of the world (John 1:29, 36). The Apostle Paul writes that "Christ died for our sins according to the scriptures" (1 Cor. 15:3); this is the final sacrifice for all of humanity. Whether viewed as the sacrificial Passover lamb in Exodus 12 who causes death to pass over people or the silent sheep who was pierced for our transgressions in Isaiah 53, his physical death on the cross provides the final atonement for humanity to be reconciled with God. It is by the death of Jesus that we are restored to God's favor. Sarah Griffith Lund (2014) writes, "The Christian witness of the cross of Jesus' death transforms this instrument of torture. Instead of only being the instrument that killed Jesus, the cross became a symbol of the power of God to overcome the sins of the world. In the resurrection, God shows us that what is broken by this world can be made whole again" (51-52). We can find new life in the loving sacrifice of Jesus. His death is not the self-aggrandizing event of a martyr, rather, it is the self-surrender of spirit that longs for the embrace of God. To suggest that his death is a suicide pollutes the reason for his death.

Interpretations of Suicide in the Bible

Historians and theologians do not agree on when the Christian Church first condemned suicide. Albert Hsu believes that the biblical accounts of suicide provide enough weight and force for us to view suicide negatively from the start. Each story is enough to see how suicide is portrayed. The biblical narrative shows us that "Suicide is never held up positively in Scripture. There are seven suicides in Scripture from King Saul to Judas, and they're always depicted negatively. They are never God's plan for anybody's life. But it's also not the unforgivable sin that automatically condemns somebody for eternity" (Hsu 2017).

Craig S. Keener (1993), for example, writes that Judas's suicide is an act of despair, but it would not be viewed well within Judaism. "Greco-Roman tradition considered suicide a nobler way to die than letting others kill one. To some Jewish people it was likewise noble if it was performed to avoid falling into the hands of torturers or to avoid being defiled. But Judaism, especially strict Palestinian Judaism, normally regarded it as evil" (124-125). Keener suggests that this Jewish understanding of suicide being wrong would automatically spill over to the followers of Jesus and Christianity because it is the default concept of the community.

Donal O'Mathuna (1998) writes that First and Second Samuel clearly teach a prohibition against suicide. You cannot evaluate the lives of those who die by suicide in the Bible without seeing their inner turmoil and troubled relationship with God. O'Mathuna says, "Following their example is contrary to divine guidance" (348). The biblical suicide accounts "support the long-standing Christian position that suicide is morally wrong" (350). Interpretation and qualification are requirements for reading scripture, especially the Old Testament. Moral instruction does not require explicit commands and edicts from scripture. O'Mathuna explains, "Rather than focusing on the abstract ethics, biblical narratives show us ethics in action in people's character. Sometimes we see godly character, sometimes ungodly"

(351). The ancient biblical texts deal with ethics in this manner. Narratives and ancient forms of literature require us to apply interpretation to each story. O'Mathuna asserts that "Problems arise when readers of the Bible fail to distinguish between God's view of what is right and 'descriptive sections of poor human responses to the lofty claims and challenges of the divine.' Just because Jews and Christians have committed suicide (recorded in the Bible or elsewhere) does not mean that Jewish or Christian teaching condones suicide" (351). The authors who condone suicide overlook the importance of this distinction when interpreting the biblical suicide accounts. They "focus on the words in the text, rather than searching for the author's intention in writing the passage" (353).

James Clemons (1990) examines all of the suicide accounts and discusses biblical references related to suicide. He looks at both sides of the theological spectrum and emphasizes the need to create a more humane and caring concern for those whose lives are touched by suicide (10). Clemons examines the biblical narrative of Saul and argues that "There is no suggestion that Saul, or even his armor-bearer, were in any way to be condemned for their actions." Clemons takes the manner of death and a lack of specific verbiage on the act to show that it "was taken simply as a normal reaction under the circumstances described" (17). He goes on to write that there is no stigma, penalty, condoning, or condemnation of suicide in any of the biblical suicide accounts. Clemons seems to hang his hat on the idea that within scripture "There are no specific injunctions against it" (30). While he does identify the need to use interpretation for reading scripture, he fails to view each story as a narrative of personal actions that shows us moral instruction.

I disagree with Clemons' point of view. He overlooks several factors in the death of King Saul and the lessons we find in scripture. First, he fails to mention that suicide is seen as a form of murder or self-murder within the Jewish community. Genesis 9:5-6 gives the Noahic covenant proscription against murder, and the Ten Commandments were in place for God's people. Unfortunately, Clemons never mentions this or any of the moral teaching already present in the Old Testament. Second, he fails to address the noble death narrative many would also ascribe to Samson. Saul lived more by secular culture than as a righteous and holy leader. His character, deeds, and actions show an early departure from God's path. Saul's suicide places culture, be it societal, military, geographic, or royal, above the example of scripture. Does his death reflect what God wants and wills for people? I do not believe so. Saul elevates the cultural noble death narrative above his God. It is just like a sea captain going down with the ship or a cancer patient refusing medication to hasten their demise. These examples place culture above the Lord. Third, Saul is selfish until the very end. He is wounded, near death, and only envisions his royal legacy being tainted. He fails to ask for heavenly intervention or seek God's favor. If there were ever a time for a flare prayer seeking God, this was it. Many scholars also overlook the fact that Saul is not alone. He has a military battle buddy at his side. Instead of asking his armor bearer to seek shelter, retreat, hide him, or to continue fighting, Saul gives up, relying on his own strength instead of the strength of God. This was the time to repent, pray, and seek the Lord. His heart was still hardened, and his final acts were purely selfish. The first king of Israel ends his life by falling on a royal sword instead of seeking out the God who anointed Saul for the throne. Clemons fails to address all of these perspectives.

Clemons (1990) believes that Christianity does not shift into condemning suicide until the time of Augustine, saying, "Voluntary martyrdom was not uncommon among the Christians of the early centuries of the church, especially in times of persecution when they faced torture or death" (26). "The fourth-century church historian Eusebius (c. 260-339/40) tells of many martyrdoms in which Christians strive to be killed, at times in spite of the entreaties of their fellow believers and even enemies" (27). Sheldrake (2007) writes that "Christianity continually confronted hostility and active persecution in the public arena until the edict of tolerance under the Emperor Constantine (313). Inevitably this gave rise to a spirituality of martyrdom related very strongly to identification with the passion of Christ" (24). The first disciples of Jesus and Stephan (Acts 7) were considered witnesses who died for the cause of Christ and were elevated in esteem for their faithful pursuit of ministry, even unto death. Sheldrake explains, "Thus martyrdom became the ultimate symbol of faithful Christian discipleship and thus of Christian holiness. More than this, the tranquil acceptance of martyrdom was an affirmation of the believer's faith in Christ's promise of victory over death and of resurrection for all who accepted the good news of God's salvation" (24).

Clemons (1990) believes early Christianity viewed suicide as acceptable martyrdom. As Christianity grew into the dominant religion of the Roman Empire, suicide was labeled a sin and a secular crime. By the fifth century, Augustine was the first Christian to make a blanket condemnation of suicide. According to Clemons, "It was probably the frequency of suicides among Christians that prompted the venerable Saint Augustine in *City of God* to offer the first systematic argument against suicide" (27). Clemons adds, "Augustine's attacks came largely in response to the heretical Donatists, and their more radical sub-group, the Circumcellions, who strongly encouraged suicide as the ultimate act of piety" (78). Many of Augustine's points were drawn from classical virtues and common sense. His most direct use of scripture however, was interpretation of the Sixth Commandment, "You shall not murder" (Exod. 20:13). In this, he interpreted suicide as self-killing or self-murder. This placed the condemnation of suicide into our religious understanding. What he likely meant as a way to preserve and promote the sanctity of life declined into legalized acts of cruelty toward suicidal people and their families, as Ramsay (2004) details: "In the Middle Ages, the criminalization of suicide was at its worst. The bodies of people who killed themselves were dragged through the streets, hung naked upside-down for public view, and impaled on a stake at a public crossroad" (20). Families were also impacted. The widow or widower and children "were formally censured, the family's property was confiscated, and the body was denied burial in the church or city cemetery" (21). Today, of 192 independent countries and states investigated, twenty-five have "specific laws and punishments for attempted suicide." Penalties in these nations range from a small fine, to short-term imprisonment, to a life sentence in prison (WHO 2014, 51).

Margaret Pabst Battin writes and defends suicide as a fundamental human right. She points out that most Western prohibitions of suicide are based on Christian arguments. Her reading and examination of scripture concludes:

> It is one of the more prevalent assumptions of Western religious culture that the Bible prohibits suicide; inspection of the biblical

texts, however, shows that this is by no means clearly the case. To begin with, there is no explicit prohibition of suicide in the Bible.... Nor is there any passage in either the Old or New Testament that can be directly understood as an explicit prohibition of suicide; those passages that are often taken to support such a prohibition require, as we shall see, a considerable amount of interpretation and qualification. (O'Matuna 1998, 350)

Battin (O'Matuna 1998) and Clemons (1990) are both correct when they identify that the word suicide is not found in the Bible. Nor is there an explicit ban on suicide. Those who condone suicide overlook the importance and necessity of interpretation. The Bible gives moral instruction by identifying good and evil actions. People normally look for a negative statement or a clear condemnation in scripture. But, the Bible expresses God's perspective in mainly positive terms. If their premise were granted, the Bible can be read to condone many other acts that are recorded without explicit condemnation. O'Mathuna gives an example from the book of Judges: "Jael killed Sisera by hammering a tent peg into his head while he slept (4:17-24). Is this then an example of what we should do to our enemies?" (353). This narrative story is given, and we can find moral instruction from it. The biblical text does not speak to this act with a parenthesis identifying it as a cold and brutal slaying, yet, we are able to clearly identify it as wrong. As a soldier myself, we are taught that there are right and wrong ways to kill an enemy. Could you not just take him prisoner? Was the tent peg a humane way to kill your opponent? This would be considered a war crime in today's understanding. It represents a cold and brutal slaying. Scripture also illustrates Joab performing a horrible and gruesome atrocity by killing Amasa. Joab stabs Amasa in such a way that his entrails literally spill onto the ground (2 Sam. 20:9-12). This would be an excruciating death. This slow and painful death is not a kosher kill or a noble way to die in battle. However, it is the third bloody murder by Joab's hand. None of these stories carries an immediate condemn or condone statement in the text. There is no need. It is not warranted. The actions speak for themselves. The ethical understanding is already understood. So it is with suicide. Suicide is wrong because it goes against the story and perspective of God throughout scripture. The biblical authors frequently give passages with no explicit ethical comment. This should not scare us. The entirety of scripture still speaks loudly on how God wants us to be his chosen people and act as righteous examples. O'Mathuna concurs: "The suicide accounts, thus interpreted, reveal a perspective on suicide consistent with the rest of Scripture" (1998, 353-354).

Battin (O'Mathuna 1998) and Clemons (1990) fall short in another area. They both fail to address the Talmudic perspective of suicide. Kaplan (2017) asserts that "No Talmudic passage can be taken as praising suicide or glorifying heroism in the Greek sense, nor is there an obsession with death as the solution to life's problems or with the issue of control" (70). Kaplan also points out the following:

> It is obviously incorrect, then, to claim that there are no suicides in biblical and later Jewish history. Individual suicides have occurred despite the injunctions against them. Nevertheless, suicide is strongly prohibited in biblical and later Jewish thought, and when it has appeared within the culture, it may represent individual idiosyncrasies, impossible external situations, or profound Greco-Roman influences. The basic Jewish preference for life over death as expressed in the Hebrew Bible has never changed, nor has suicide ever been idealized as an end in itself. (71)

Even the fall of Masada should be seen with this lens. "Although Masada has become a symbol of bravery in much of the modern world, its lesson for Israel is that Masada must not fall again, rather than the aggrandizement of suicide" (70). Ignoring the Jewish perspective on suicide weakens their arguments and works to conceal a scriptural understanding on the subject. We can read the proscription of suicide in the text without a specific condone or condemn statement beside each example of suicide.

Suicide and Salvation

This is a controversial topic that can quickly turn emotional. There are also several points of view within Christianity, and I believe a biblical analysis is the best way to address the matter of salvation and suicide. The theological issue can be divided into two predominant perspectives. One group believes that suicide is a mortal sin that irretrievably sends people to Hell. The mortal sin position is found in the Roman Catholic Church. The second group believes that suicide is a sin but does not elevate one sin above another. All sins are equally bad and offensive to God, but they are all capable of being forgiven through the atoning sacrifice of Jesus. This is the predominant view of evangelical Christians and most of the Protestant community. I will include Roman Catholic creeds, statements of faith, and historical perspective to examine their theology. I will not use creedal statements or a catechism in the Protestant section because of the furcated nature it would take in Protestant circles. This group universally believes in the authority of scripture and uses the Bible to establish their position. Scripture will be the focus through which to examine their theology.

The Roman Catholic Approach

The Roman Catholic Church views suicide as a mortal sin, maintaining a distinction between mortal and venial sins. The former separates us from God's grace; the latter, while serious, does not. The Catechism of the Catholic Church (CCC) states:

> Mortal sin is a radical possibility of human freedom, as is love itself. It results in the loss of charity and the privation of sanctifying grace, that is, of the state of grace. If it is not redeemed by repentance and God's forgiveness, it causes exclusion from Christ's kingdom and the eternal death of hell, for our freedom has the power to make choices forever, with no turning back. However, although we can judge that an act is in itself a grave offense, we must entrust judgment of persons to the justice and mercy of God. (2019, 1861)

The Roman Catholic position believes that deliberately taking your own life annihilates all that you possess of the spiritual life, since suicide is an absolute contradiction to everything that Christianity believes and teaches. Catholics raised with the Baltimore Catechism (BC) were taught that suicide is a mortal sin because it is an act against the will of God and a violation of the fifth commandment. Protestants count the edict against murder as the sixth commandment, while Roman Catholics count it as the fifth. The Baltimore

Catechism asks, "What sin is it to destroy one's own life, or commit suicide, as this act is called?" The catechism answer is, "It is a mortal sin to destroy one's own life or commit suicide, as this act is called, and persons who willfully and knowingly commit such an act die in a state of mortal sin and are deprived of Christian burial. It is also wrong to expose oneself unnecessarily to the danger of death by rash or foolhardy feats of daring" (BC 1274). They use scripture and tradition to teach that suicide costs someone his or her salvation. While this teaching has not exactly changed, it has become more nuanced.

A person who willfully and knowingly chooses suicide would still be considered to be in a state of mortal sin. The Roman Catholic Church acknowledges, however, that most people who die by suicide suffer from mental illness and are thus incapable of making a clear, rational decision. This was first reflected in 1992 when John Paul II approved a change to the Catechism of the Catholic Church. This newly articulated position represents a major move for the Roman Catholic stance on suicide. When you consider that the needle barely moved since the time of Augustine, this new position can be likened to a sea change. It was truly a historic event. The Catechism of the Catholic Church (2019) even highlights the 1992 portion by setting it apart from the original section in statement 2282:

Suicide

2280 Everyone is responsible for his life before God who has given it to him. It is God who remains the sovereign Master of life. We are obliged to accept life gratefully and preserve it for his honor and the salvation of our souls. We are stewards, not owners, of the life God has entrusted to us. It is not ours to dispose of.

2281 Suicide contradicts the natural inclination of the human being to preserve and perpetuate his life. It is gravely contrary to the just love of self. It likewise offends love of neighbor because it unjustly breaks the ties of solidarity with family, nation, and other human societies to which we continue to have obligations. Suicide is contrary to love for the living God.

2282 If suicide is committed with the intention of setting an example, especially to the young, it also takes on the gravity of scandal. Voluntary co-operation in suicide is contrary to the moral law.

Grave psychological disturbances, anguish, or grave fear of hardship, suffering, or torture can diminish the responsibility of the one committing suicide.

2283 We should not despair of the eternal salvation of persons who have taken their own lives. By ways known to him alone, God can provide the opportunity for salutary repentance. The Church prays for persons who have taken their own lives. (CCC 2019)

The catechism affirms that suicide is contrary to both love of God and love of self and that it goes against the basic human instinct to preserve life. However, it also notes that "Grave psychological disturbances, anguish, or grave fear of hardship, suffering, or torture can diminish the responsibility of the one committing suicide" (2282). This new understanding establishes a bright line showing a moral difference between volitional suicide and suicide due to psychological or physiological factors, such as a chemical imbalance, clinical depression, or a mental illness. I agree that there is a difference between volitional suicide and suicide due to mental illness. Mental illness is a biochemical reality of our fallen nature. Some forms of severe mental illness cannot be prevented. Treatment can mitigate the psychological and physical nature of mental illness and provide symptom management, but some forms of mental illness cannot be prevented or cured. Mental illness is a disease, a genetic and biological reality. Some people will never have the ability to make rational choices because of their affliction. More denominations with the Christian faith are beginning to embrace this position.

The catechism also emphasizes that the church should pray for those who die by suicide and should not fear for their eternal salvation. This addition captures the idea that there is ultimately no telling if the person might have repented split seconds before death. The last catechism statement on suicide also encourages us with, "We should not despair of the eternal salvation of persons who have taken their own lives. By ways known to him alone, God can provide the opportunity for salutary repentance" (2283). Catholics believe that all sins must be confessed to regain the grace of God, since it is lost by sin. Catholics must confess venial sins and mortal sins to receive reconciliation with God and the church. In their view, unconfessed sin could potentially change one's eternal home. In the case of suicide, Catholics advance the possibility that in the process of dying one might regret his or her action and repent of it, calling for God's mercy. God can transcend time, so it is possible for his grace to be extended even in the moments just before death. Monsignor Charles Pope (2018) explains that in dying, there are some obvious physical qualities, but there is also latitude for some mysterious aspects related to the spirit's full departure to the judgment seat of Christ. Pope says, "It is to these mysteries that the Catechism refers. The same could be said for those who die suddenly. There may be some moments after physical death, but prior to the soul's departure where repentance is still possible" (2018). Salutary repentance is something that only God can give. The how is not known or even taught by the Church. It is totally in God's hands. Did the suicidal person willfully separate himself or herself from God by his or her own free choice? Jesus will see the truth of the matter and judge accordingly.

The Roman Catholic position on salutary repentance and the Almighty's ultimate sovereignty leave room for God to act with grace and mercy as the final judge. I personally like this because it places God above any denomination's religious rulebook. It also points out that clergy must never condemn a victim of suicide to Hell but always have hope in the power of God's mercy. God alone knows the depth of each person, and he would never allow a person to perish without the full benefit of his mercy. Monsignor Pope reminds his readers, "Scripture frequently warns of the need to be ready well before death. Many of Jesus' parables speak of his sudden coming and that there are some who are ready and some who are not.... Hence, we should trust and hope in God's mercy but not lightly presume upon it such that we disregard Jesus' teachings and warnings" (Pope 2018).

The Protestant Approach

Evangelical Christians and most Protestants do not believe it is possible for a Christian to lose his or her salvation, even if that person dies by suicide. Yes, suicide is a sin among many sins, but it does not cast one away from the atoning work of Jesus. This camp makes no distinction or division on sin. The sin of suicide cannot be excluded or divided into another category, because there is only one category. The Protestant position also takes the tact that even after regeneration a Christian is capable of committing any sin. A believer could even take the life of someone else, as Moses and David did, without this action invalidating their salvation. The sacrificial atonement of Jesus is made by his death on the cross. This action has forgiven all of our sins – past, present, and future (Heb. 10:11-18). This one offering makes us clean through the blood of Jesus, as stated in Hebrews: "For by one offering He has perfected for all time those who are sanctified" (10:14). It is the fulfillment of Jeremiah 31:34 when God declares, "And their sins and their lawless deeds I will remember no more." The sin a Christian commits tomorrow was already forgiven at the cross of Christ. Jesus justifies the believer, making us positionally righteous (Rom. 3:23-26; 8:29-30). The Protestant believes that Jesus' death is capable of forgiving any sin.

Protestants also point out that a Christian is forever a child of God. Eternal life is bestowed on the believer. As Jesus said, we are born again, enabling entry to see and partake in the kingdom of God (John 3:3). Our immortality is in the present tense. It is right now. This is unlike the Roman Catholic position, which claims that one can forfeit their salvation or that the Holy Spirit somehow leaves the human body with the commission of suicide. Suicide is not apostasy. The Bible assures us with, "I write these things to you who believe in the name of the Son of God so that you may know that you have eternal life" (1 John 5:13). We become subjects in the kingdom of God. We are on Earth but are partakers of the eternal life that Christ proclaims. We are part of the family of God, as declared in John 3:16: "For God so loved the world, that He gave His only begotten Son, that whoever believes in him shall not perish, but have eternal life." We become a new creation, one that will live on in union with God. Jesus said, "I am the resurrection and the life; he who believes in Me will live even if he dies, and everyone who lives and believes in Me will never die" (John 11:25-26).

Lastly, suicide is not the unforgivable sin that separates us from God. Those who die by suicide do not automatically go to Hell because of the act. Protestants balk hard at this idea because it creates a transactional view of sin and forgiveness, one wherein forgiveness is earned or received by our own meritorious acts. The idea of a Christian going to Hell because of suicide would mean that his or her salvation was a work undone by the act of suicide. Suicide somehow becomes stronger than the death and resurrection of Jesus. No verse of scripture cancels the atonement of Jesus. No verse of scripture connects suicide with our eternal destiny. If this act could cause us to lose our salvation, then the Bible would make that clear. We cannot earn or lose our salvation by human actions. Suicide does not separate the believer from the Savior. Grace and mercy cannot be earned by our earthly actions, as stated in Ephesians: "For by grace you have been saved through faith; and that not of yourselves, it is the gift of God; not as a result of works, so that no one may boast" (2:8-9). Meritorious works do not save us. Poor works do not condemn us. Wrong acts, deeds, and works cannot cancel our salvation in Christ. Human actions do not cancel our positional righteousness, the righteousness we receive from God through Christ. The Bible tells us that once we are in Christ, nothing can separate us from Him (Rom. 8:35-39). Once a you become a Christian, God will always be your Father. If you ask Jesus Christ to be your Lord, nothing can take you from His hand (John 10:28). The unpardonable sin is rejecting the Holy Spirit's offer of salvation and dying in a state of that rejection (Matt. 12:31). It is refusing the only pardon God is able to give. The act of suicide is not the unforgivable sin and does not cancel our salvation in Jesus Christ. We must continue to share this theological position with others, because it reveals the depth and richness of God's love.

Discovering Hope

The Bible is the Word of Life. It has much to say about redemption, sharing hope, and endurance. Faith is viewed as a protective factor from suicide for a reason. We all experience dark days that require reminders of hope. The Bible offers many valuable verses on strength and support that encourage us to be strong in our faith and our daily walk with God. I believe that these passages can help shine the light of Christ into some of the darkest places and times of our lives. Jesus promised, "I am with you always, even to the end of the age" (Matt. 28:20b). While these closing words of Matthew were given to the disciples, they affirm the Christian idea that Jesus Christ is always present in the lives of the faithful. We all need to hear this reminder, but people suffering with suicidal thoughts may need to hear the promise even more. There is incredible power knowing that Christ is with me and will not abandon me. Hebrews 13:5 echoes this idea, stating, "For he has said, 'I will never leave you or forsake you.'" We also hear the Psalmist share that "God is our refuge and strength, an ever-present help in trouble" (Ps. 46:11). There are times when people need a reminder that they are not alone. People at risk of suicide can feel isolated and withdrawn, making passages like this a balm for relief and comfort.

Endurance passages teach us resilience and how to grow from hardship. Peter 1:6-9 says that, for a little while, we may suffer various trials, but the outcome is salvation of our souls. Second Corinthians, chapter 4 tells us to not lose heart, a frequent message in this chapter. The power that directs us is from above. It is beyond our earthly bodies, which Paul compares to clay jars with a tremendous treasure on the inside: "But we have this treasure in jars of clay to show that this all-surpassing power is from God and not from us. We are hard-pressed on every side, but not crushed; perplexed, but not in despair; persecuted, but not abandoned; struck down, but not destroyed" (2 Cor. 4:8-9). There is difficulty, but we are not defeated. There is hardship, but we are never overwhelmed. God will get us through the darkest and harshest storm. Colossians 2:6-7 encourages us to be firm and rooted in our Savior: "As you therefore have received Christ Jesus the Lord, continue to live your lives in him, rooted and built up in him and established in the faith, just as you were taught, abounding in thanksgiving." Just like a century-old oak tree, deep roots will produce a strong faith that can endure the storms of life. Hebrews 10:35-36 offers this assurance: "Therefore, do not throw away your confidence, which has a great reward. For you have need of endurance, so that when you have done the will of God, you may receive what was promised." Just like the refiner's fire, we must stay strong through any tribulation. Enduring the heat of the furnace removes the dross and impurities to create a stronger and valuable product. Suffering can form us into a stronger person. We eventually come out of the trial in better condition to do the work of God. Christianity acknowledges the emptiness and brokenness of the world and offers hope and life through Jesus.

CHAPTER 4
SPIRITUAL PRACTICES

The Benefits of Religion

Professional and scientific psychology have rediscovered religion. Thomas Plante (2007) notes:

> While a number of our prominent psychology forefathers such as William James, Carl Jung, and Gordon Allport were keenly interested in the relationship between psychology and religion (e.g., Allport, 1950; James, 1890, 1902; Jung, 1938), most of professional and scientific psychology during the past century has avoided the connection between these two areas of inquiry. (891-892)

Plante suggests that the discipline tended to "shy away from all things religious or spiritual in an effort to maximize and emphasize the rigorous scientific approach to both research and clinical practice" (892). Since much of religion and spirituality could not be considered observable or measurable, many just wanted to avoid all aspects of faith. This desire, combined with some hostile attitudes toward religion, allowed psychology to throw the baby out with the bath water.[10] As a result, religion and the behavioral sciences operated independently of each other for a very long time. There was little if any integration between the disciplines. They mostly stayed within their own spheres of influence and moved forward without integration or attempts to heal the old rifts and divisions. Many individuals found this arrangement comfortable, while others sought détente. Eventually, this miniature cold war between church and clinic thawed out. Scientific advances and movement toward holistic health models have played a large part in advancing integration. As methods and understanding grew, the fields of religion and psychology have realigned. Plante says:

> Toward the very end of the 20th century, psychology (as well as science in general) has embraced spirituality and religion more and

has used rigorous scientific methods such as double-blind randomized clinical trials to examine important questions related to psychology and religion integration (Miller, 1999; Miller & Thoresen, 2003; Plante & Sherman, 2001). These include the influence of religious and spiritual behaviors and beliefs on both mental and physical health outcomes (Koenig, McCullough, & Larson, 2001; Pargament, 1997; Plante & Sharma, 2001). In recent years, spirituality, religion, psychology, and science integration has been legitimized. (892)

We can even see how the church moved closer to the field of psychology during this time of realignment. Lund (2014) points this out:

There is good news about the positive role of churches breaking the silence about mental illness. In the spring of 2014, megachurch pastor and *Purpose Driven Life* author Rick Warren hosted the largest gathering of Christians (three thousand in attendance, with thousands more participating online) for a conference about mental illness. (96-97)

Plante concurs: "Several training programs often associated with evangelical Protestant churches did emerge that freely embraced and nurtured religion and psychological integration" (892). This trend continues today as churches hold sessions, workshops, and training events on the importance of mental health and suicide prevention (Bates 2019).

Today, conferences, seminars, workshops, and multiple journals attest to the importance of integrating religion and psychology. Plante (2007) says, "Journals such as the *American Psychologist*, *Annals of Behavioral Medicine*, and *Journal of Health Psychology*, among others, have recently dedicated special issues to this important topic" (891). Professional organizations, such as the Society of Behavioral Medicine, have developed special interest groups, task forces, and committees that focus on the integration of religion and health (892). Multiple research entities, such as the John Templeton, Lily, and Fetzer Foundations and government agencies, such as the National Institute of Health, have funded and continue to support large-scale projects on the physical and mental health benefits of religion and spirituality (892-893). It appears that the integration of psychology with religion and spirituality is certainly stronger than where it started.

William P. Wilson is a psychiatrist with the Duke University Medical Center. He was one of the first researchers in psychiatry to publish on religion and mental health in mainstream medical and psychiatric journals. He emphasizes approaches that honor the body, mind, and spirit aspects for total wellness and healing. He also writes to bring a greater clinical understanding of how religion can be applied to different disciplines for application, study, and research, saying, "I must point out that humans are more than biopsychosocial beings. They are biopsychosociospiritual beings. If humans have a spiritual component then it follows that they can have spiritual disease." Here, Wilson identifies human beings as patients with the spiritual disease of "being unregenerate" and the "disease of sin," like any syndromes that need treatment. If therapists, clinicians, and physicians accept that these "diseases are spiritual in etiology, it stands to reason that spiritual interventions might be of benefit in treating them." In Christianity, a spiritual intervention would likely utilize prayer; bibliotherapy; confession, repentance, and forgiveness; exhortation; affirmation; and worship, including the Eucharist (Wilson 1998, 162). Spiritual therapy can facilitate the help and healing that people need.

Wilson strongly believes in the need for integration, observing that early studies noted how religious experiences have pervasively affected the personality of people who have gone through them (1998, 162). Wilson writes that "Empirical evidence discovered by these early pioneers in the field demonstrated that religious experiences can be truly life changing, and even the Group for the Advancement of Psychiatry (1968) attested to the dramatic effects of religious conversion on the personality" (162). Religion and spirituality can change us in many positive ways. They influence our spiritual, mental, and physical health. Religious practices influence our faith and our total wellness. Wilson firmly believes that religion must have a seat at the table to influence total wellness for everyone (Koenig 1998).

According to Koenig (1998) in *The Handbook of Religion and Mental Health*, "Religiosity is a clear stress deterrent and also impacts depression rates" (27).

Religion is a strong protective factor against suicide and provides protective benefits for our total wellness. Koenig says, "Religiosity indicators are especially significant as coping resources" (27). Over fifty-eight years ago, Srole and Langer, researchers from the seminal Midtown Manhattan Study (1962) compared the prevalence of mental illness among active and currently "unchurched" Catholics, Protestants, and Jews. Koenig continues, "They found higher ratios of impaired to well respondents among currently nonaffiliated from all three religious groups, in comparison with such ratios among respondents still active in the religion of origin" (Koenig 1998, 36). This early study helped open the spigot and create a stronger showing for religion and spirituality in multiple fields of health. Today, studies continue to show positive outcomes with more sophisticated methods and models. As you find early and modern work, the studies continue to suggest that "Religious involvement exhibits both preventative and therapeutic effects on mental health outcomes" (36).

Religion and spirituality also form greater resilience in people. Resiliency can be understood as the ability to bounce back from tough times, hardships, and difficulties. Gang Wu (2013) highlights a study on the resiliency of 121 outpatients with depression and or anxiety disorder. The study showed that "A low or lack of purpose in life and less frequent physical exercise were correlated with low resilience, but low spirituality prevailed as a leading predictor of low resilience" (7). Little religion and spirituality meant little resiliency. Trials and tribulations are viewed in a different light by those who have and rely on their faith.

Natalia Yangarber-Hicks (2006) sees remarkable progress in this integration, claiming, "The pursuit of integration between Christian faith and psychology in the last 50 years has produced much fruit despite the lingering lack of consensus regarding definitions of the integration enterprise, criteria for determining truth, and future directions." She suggests that psychologists and Christians can find universal agreement in one area: future generations of those committed to integration have much work left to do. She shares that the current field of literature requires more voices and perspectives on Christian psychology to be present and actively engaged at the integration table (338). She adds:

> Psychologically valid descriptions of Christianity as it is lived can enrich our understanding of how to best carry out Christian ministry in a broad range of contexts. In turn, a better understanding of religious processes in psychological terms can influence the development of more general psychological models (347).

If the last half century is an accurate guide, the next fifty years will provide even more integration and awareness of how religion and spirituality can benefit our wellbeing.

Religiosity is an incredible deterrent to suicide, suicidal behavior, and suicidal ideation. Clinical epidemiology shows religious and spiritual (R/S) engagement to be the leading protective factor conferring prevention against suicide. In a meta-analytic study of 2,339 completed suicides and 5,252 matched controls, Andrew Wu and his colleagues showed a 71% protective benefit of R/S within Western traditions and 81% when further R/S is shared in a community (2015, 1). Those figures show the inherent strength of religion and spirituality protecting people against suicide. In fact, it is hard to find evidence of a stronger protective factor. Parental religious beliefs can also be counted as assets in the war against suicide. According to Connie Svob (2018), religion and spirituality can be scientifically documented as a protective factor against suicide through parenting children. Even among adults at high heritable and family risk for depression and suicide, there exists an 80% decreased risk for suicidal ideation and/or behavior if raised by a parent with a high level of R/S (1062). There is no protective factor identified by the clinical sciences in scope or scale that compares to the protective benefits of religion and spirituality against suicide.

In 2019, a study was written to evaluate if nonreligious individuals have the same mental health and wellbeing benefits as religious individuals. Specifically, it investigates the research findings that use Christian and secular samples to explore the relationship between religiosity and mental health. Park (2019) suggests, "Research in this area suffers from many weaknesses, including heavy dependence on self-report measures and cross-sectional studies, problems with defining religion and spirituality, and too much dependence on Christian samples." Park and her fellow study authors are concerned with the assumption that religious individuals are more often joyful and positive than nonreligious individuals. The authors share, "We also hope to instill a degree of caution about drawing overly optimistic conclusions about the benefits of faith" (81). They are concerned that the pendulum has swung too far in the direction of religion and that a majority of literature is overly outweighed with its benefits (84). They also want to ensure that strict and accurate methods are used in studies to evaluate religion and spirituality.

The researchers created a sophisticated matrix to examine and evaluate empirical research studies based on their hypothesis. The matrix required a group of religious and nonreligious participants, using quantitative measures on religiosity, along with integral data and categorical data. Their manner of research would weed out the weaker samplings and allow experts to examine the best studies currently in the field. The concluding results show that two-thirds of these identified studies found significant benefits for religious individuals (Park 2019, 89):

> Review of these studies indicates that religious individuals experience greater mental health benefits than nonreligious individuals. Two-thirds of the studies we identified documented positive benefits for religious individuals, a fraction that parallels the reports of Koenig et al. (2012). We concur with other research documenting that religious individuals do accrue mental health benefits that nonreligious individuals on average do not accrue. (92)

Even the strongest research methods and screenings show that religion makes us stronger people. People who practice and engage their faith have greater health outcomes and benefits than those who do not have a faith background. Koenig (1998) is not alone in demonstrating the benefits of religion and spirituality.

Studies continue to show the positive effects of R/S. Robins (2009) says, "People with higher levels of religious involvement are at decreased risk of suicide compared to people who are not religious or whose level of religious involvement is lower" (386). Some conjecture exists on how this bears out in research. Do certain religious beliefs offer protection from suicide? Do certain public and private religious practices offer protection from suicide? Sometimes, the term religiousness has been used to refer to the general characteristic of adhering to a set of religious beliefs or practices shared by a group. Numerous aspects of religiousness or religiosity have been investigated. While "Evidence supports the conclusion that religiousness is associated with lower levels of suicidal ideation, suicide attempts, and even death by suicide," Robins says that the association is often attributed to religious beliefs (387).

The 2009 Alee Robins and Amy Fiske study shows that "Engaging in public religious practices was related to lower levels of suicidal ideation and suicide attempts," and according to Robins, social support also mediates the relationship (392). Public religious practices were measured by attendance at worship services and other religious activities using the Organizational Religiousness Form from the National Institute on Aging Workgroup, an arm of the National Institutes of Health. Measuring attendance is often done to determine religiousness. The Fetzer Institute (2003) comments that "Frequency of attendance at services may indicate the frequency with which heightened states of religious consciousness or the experience of the sacred is achieved through prayer, music, architecture, or rituals" (76). Utilizing the Organizational Religiousness Form also measures attending religious activities at church: praying; singing, performing, or listening to music; reading or listening to scripture; hearing sermons; conducting rituals and sacraments; and sitting in silence (76-78). The big conclusion from the 2009 study shows that these public spiritual practices reduce suicidal thoughts and suicide attempts.

Since the nineteenth century, sociologists like Émile Durkheim have pointed to religion as a protective factor against suicide. According to De La Vega Sanchez (2020), research shows the following:

> Religious affiliation has been associated with protection against both suicidal behavior and self-harm. Religious believers also have a lower incidence of risk factors for suicidal behavior such as substance abuse or depressive disorders. The bulk of this protection appears

to depend not on the specific religious denomination, but on the degree of involvement or its importance in daily life (2).

The greater involvement and importance of religion in one's life can be classified as a measurable way to combat suicide. Seeing spiritual practices as tools and resources that Christians use in the involvement of their faith bears out these findings. Using spiritual practices daily would fit the framework to reduce suicidal risk. Daily religious activities strengthen the protective dam that holds back suicidal ideation and suicidal behavior. Going through the motions just for the sake of religious obligation does not yield the same impact against suicide. Engaging your faith with higher degrees of involvement and importance does make an impact against suicide. De La Vega Sanchez goes on to share study results that found "A tendency toward deterioration of religiosity has been described occurring one year before a suicide attempt" (2). Moving away from faith and religious involvement hurts our wellbeing. When R/S involvement and importance fall, the protective dam softens and may cause a break, allowing suicidal thoughts and behavior to overwhelm an individual.

In an epidemiological study of 16,795 deaths, including 1,385 suicides, research led by Steven Stack (2018) found that a one-unit increase in religious activity equaled a 17% reduction in the odds of suicide among males and a 15% reduction among females. This particular study showed, "the greater the reported religious activities, the lower the risk of death by suicide." The finding was true for both men and women (4). While all studies do not show these results, it is important to highlight the findings of the 2018 project by Stack. Many studies measure or limit religiosity to the presence or lack of a declared religious preference. These projects only look to see if one identifies with a particular religion or faith group. The projects do not detail or evaluate the level of religious involvement or activity. The Stack study makes religious activity a key component of its work and uses it in a scientific manner to differentiate levels of religiosity that many studies do not examine. The religious activity index also showed that "Women are more religious than men," and this level of religiosity "may protect women more than men against suicide."[11] Again, the main takeaway was that religious activity lowers the risk of suicide in people. This finding should not be overlooked. Stack shows us that "Religious activities protect both men and women from suicide deaths. The extent to which religiousness protects against suicide is essentially the same for males and females" (8). While many studies conclude that "Being more religious correlates with low suicidality" (Waitz-Kudla 2019, 1514), the Stack study raises the bar by demonstrating that religious activities reduce the chances of death by suicide.

A growing body of literature has explored the relationship between R/S and our wellbeing. Mounting evidence in research, studies, and papers concludes that R/S benefits our mental and physical health. Past studies have shown that religious affiliation, holding religious beliefs, and considering religion to be personally important to have lowered the risk of suicidal behavior. Now there is a growing trend in the literature to suggest that something may be linked more strongly to the benefits of R/S, like religious involvement and activity. The last three studies mentioned point this out as a measurable conclusion. Religious involvement and activity demonstrate a strong protective factor against suicide that is difficult to deny. It lowers suicidal ideation and suicidal behavior for individuals who actively engage their faith. The 2009 Robins and Fiske study even identified the specific spiritual practices that can measurably reduce suicidal risk, such as attending worship services; participating in religious activities; prayer; singing, performing, or listening to worship music; studying scripture; hearing sermons; conducting rituals and sacraments; and sitting in silence (Robins & Fiske, 392 and Fetzer, 76). Using these spiritual practices and disciplines shows evidence of reducing suicidal thoughts and actions.

Although the behavioral scientific studies of religion and spirituality acknowledge vast benefits for those contemplating suicide, Christians believe that God is the ultimate source of the benefits. God may work many ways to comfort, encourage, guide, and empower people facing life-threatening challenges. Among those ways are spiritual practices that people – Christians and non-Christians alike – undertake with the expectation of God's gracious enablement. They serve as ways of "planting" and "watering" people's growth in the midst of crises. Of course, it is not the spiritual practices that ultimately bring the growth; it is God. As the apostle Paul says, "I planted, Apollos watered, but God gave the growth" (1 Cor. 3:6). In the context of his letter to the Corinthians, Paul contributed to their spiritual "planting," and another apostle named Apollos contributed to their spiritual "watering." Paul understood that responding well to life's challenges involves human cooperation with God's grace in producing the kind of maturation that helps people persevere and flourish in the midst of trials and temptations. Let us now turn to a discussion of Christian spiritual practices, especially as they relate to those considering the prospect of suicide.

Understanding Spiritual Practices

In this section, I will discuss the use of Christian spiritual practices that people use for spiritual growth and formation. Authors, pastors, and theologians use additional terms for these practices, such as Christian practices, spiritual disciplines, spiritual exercises, religious practices, rituals, or the disciplines. I will use the terms spiritual disciplines, spiritual practices, and/or spiritual exercises interchangeably to identify the religious rituals and practices that foster spiritual growth and spiritual formation. Spiritual growth through prescribed disciplines is not new. These disciplines are ancient practices found in the Bible and across Christianity. Some denominations are just discovering the disciplines in order to foster spiritual growth in people. You can identify these churches that are finding spiritual disciplines. They are like one traveling in a wooded thicket that appears overgrown and abandoned. The weeds and brush are thick. At first, it appears that no one has travelled this way before. But, the farther you walk, your journey eventually brings you to a well-worn and established path. What seemed hidden or lost has, in fact, been there for over fifteen centuries. It was just waiting for you to discover it and begin your journey. Spiritual direction, spiritual growth, and spiritual formation are biblical concepts frequently associated with Christian terms like discipleship, shepherding, leading, guiding, and teaching. They are long-established paths that move us closer to God.

To understand the value of spiritual disciplines, consider the importance of relationships. The amount of time, listening, conversation, and honesty we share with another shows the depth and desire we have for that relationship. It is this way with our families and friends, and, according to Dallas Willard, so it is with God. Willard says, "God has created us for intimate friendship with himself – both now and forever. This is the Christian viewpoint" (1999, 10). We find this throughout scripture. God is in conversation with Adam, Eve, Enoch, Abraham, Moses, King David, and the prophets. We often lift up these historical heroes of the faith and classify their relationship with God as exceptional. In many evangelical circles, they stand on pillars too high for us to reach. However, they were not meant to be exceptional. Willard says, "Rather they are examples of the normal human life God intended for us: God's indwelling his people through personal presence and fellowship" (18). Just as God spoke to Adam and Eve, the first people of creation, he speaks to all of his people. Psalm 145:18-19 states, "The Lord is near to all who call on him, to all who call on him in truth. He fulfills the desire of those who fear him, he also hears their cry and saves them." God has not stopped talking, nor has his care for us waned.

God still desires a relationship with all of his people. This original intent has never fallen away. Community, fellowship, and togetherness are still vital for our faith and us. We are not meant to live in isolation, and scripture confirms that it is not good for us to be alone (Gen. 2:18). We were never designed to be alone. Adele Calhoun (2015) says, "God created us for community and interdependence – with the Trinity and with others. God is never alone. The Holy One is Trinity. And we are created in this interdependent image. We need others" (143). Calhoun's observation on the Trinity is quite amazing. God is always in relationship, because God is Trinity and constantly in relationship. As we are created in God's image, so that importance of relationship is passed on to us. Many people outside of the church feel this desire for relationship but do not know how to give it voice. They seek an alternative spirituality that mimics compassion but is not built on the love of Jesus. The power of affective prayer is love. Robin Maas (1990) says, "Eventually we reach the point in a close relationship where we do not always have to find something to do or say; we can simply be quietly together. The same holds true for our relationship with God" (260).

Our personal relationship with God is key to conversation. The relationship can wither on the vine or be completely ignored. Willard reveals that our "Failure to hear God has its deepest roots in a failure to understand, accept, and grow into a conversational relationship with God, the sort of relationship suited to friends who are mature personalities in a shared enterprise, no matter how different they may be in other respects" (Willard 1999, 29). When people fail to engage and practice their faith, it impedes their relationship with the Almighty. People often search for God, because they are not close to God. The familiarity has been lost or is unknown, but we can always return to our Father. One may even think that he or she is not that important or worthy to talk with God. These thoughts are common misconceptions that shut us off from the gracious and loving relationship God desires with us. The truth is that God does consider us that important. We are so important that God gave his Son's life for us and chooses to live in us as the indwelt Holy Spirit. What greater signs of importance could there be?

Father William Barry believes that spiritual exercises and practices should be viewed as ways for us to build our relationship with God. God invites us into the relational life. Barry says, "God is always acting to bring about this intention" (1991, 14). During every moment of our existence, God is communicating to us and trying to draw us near. God is always present. God is constant and available. Barry continues, "Whether we are aware of it or not, at every moment of our existence we are encountering God, Father, Son, and Holy Spirit, who is trying to catch our attention, trying to draw us into a reciprocal conscious relationship" (14-15). The disciplines are a way to seek a deeper relationship and a closer walk with God. This perspective emphasizes that spiritual exercises are for everyone. We are all invited to participate and engage God in relationship. The call to participate is for all. Disciplines are for everybody. The exercises are not reserved for the super religious, monks, or those in a religious order, but for all people. Barry believes that spiritual exercises "are any means by which we come into contact with God: means to overcome our resistances and to relate to God and of discerning in our experience what is of God and what is not of God" (14).

The desire to know and love God fuels spiritual exercises. Calhoun (2015) writes, "From its beginning the church linked the desire for more of God to intentional practices, relationships and experiences that gave people space in their lives to 'keep company' with Jesus. These intentional practices, relationships and exercises we know as spiritual disciplines." (19) The Book of Acts outlines the apostles of Jesus utilizing spiritual exercises of compassion, intercession, service, prayer, fasting, discernment, and worship. Later, in the fourth and fifth centuries, the desert fathers and mothers found that the politicized and anemic nature of the church had caused many to forget their first love. They moved away from the urban centers and into the remote boundaries where they could show greater intention to collaborate with God. Calhoun says, "Their longing to be conformed to the image of Christ gave rise to spiritual disciplines of silence, solitude, contemplation, spiritual direction and detachment" (19). It is important to note that spiritual exercises were never considered meritorious works but, rather, a way to grow our relationship with God. People collaborate with God's Spirit through the prevenient workings of divine grace by which God gives growth (1 Cor. 3:6). Seeing the disciplines as a way to keep company with Jesus is a helpful path to grow and develop our relationship.

Scripture

Scripture allows us to see Jesus using several spiritual disciplines. Jesus specifically used scripture, prayer, silence, solitude, fasting, and worship. He learned, studied, and memorized scripture. The Bible (Hebrew scripture) was the only book Jesus quoted. He did not use it for discussion but, rather, to decide the point of numerous issues. Jesus knew scripture better than anyone else did. As a boy, he amazed the teachers in Jerusalem with his understanding (Luke 2:46-47). He quoted scripture from memory when tempted in the wilderness (Luke 4:1-13). Each of the three times Satan tried to tempt our Lord, Jesus replied with, "It is written" and declare a scriptural text from the Book of Deuteronomy (Matt. 4:4, 7, 10). All of these examples are commandments that Israel failed to obey in the wilderness, but Jesus is determined to obey. Jesus' first citation declared the primacy of God's words for us. He said, "Man shall not live on bread alone, but on every word that comes from the mouth of God" (Matt. 4:4). It is the true food or meal that empowers us for life. It feeds our spirit and strengthens our faith. This is a stark contrast to Satan's abuse and manipulation of scripture. Here, Jesus emphasizes scripture's power when rightly interpreted and applied.

We also see Jesus quoting and referencing scripture in His teaching (Matt. 5:21; Mark 10:5-9). Jesus used scripture to teach God's will. David said in Psalm 16:8, "I keep the Lord always before me." The best way to keep the Lord before us can be seen as knowing scripture. Dallas Willard believed that "Bible memorization is absolutely fundamental to spiritual formation. If I had to . . . choose between all the disciplines of the spiritual life and take only one, I would choose Bible memorization" (2006, 58). He saw a deep knowledge of scripture as the necessary way to fill our minds with the lessons and examples of God. All four gospels in the New Testament show Jesus using scripture and explaining it in a way that was new to the audience. The crowds were often amazed at how Jesus taught lessons from scripture. They heard lessons that emphasized love, grace, and mercy. They discovered teaching focused on kingdom principles and ethics. They found instructions for life instead of just following the law out of obligation. Jesus used scripture to enlighten and educate people instead of using it as a way to burden people with strict rules, as the Pharisees did.

The instruction of scripture is vital. There is no substitute for the knowledge and insight we gain from the text. Nothing people write about the Bible can be on the same level with the actual Word of God. We study the Bible to know the God of the Bible. We learn to be holy and righteous people in the way of Jesus. The Holy Spirit is also at work to open our hearts and minds to the divine message of God. Spiritual maturity is not measured by our knowledge of obscure Bible facts or trivia. The fruit of the spirit being abundantly evident in our lives measures it. When the Bible takes root in us, then we are known by how we reflect God.

Prayer

As important as the study of scripture is, Jesus practiced other disciplines, which are crucial to our spiritual well-being. Mark 1:35 records, "In the early morning, while it was still dark, Jesus got up, left the house, and went away to a secluded place, and was praying there." This one verse shows Jesus practicing three separate spiritual disciplines: prayer, silence, and solitude. Jesus taught many things about prayer. He cautioned followers "not to be like the hypocrites" or to "use meaningless repetition as the Gentiles do" but to instead "Go into your inner room, close your door and pray to your Father who is in secret" (Matt. 6:5; 6:7; 6:6). This last point on prayer can often be overlooked, but Jesus often emphasized separation during prayer. He would withdraw for time alone with God in prayer. We also see Jesus getting away from the crowds to pray in solitude and silence (Matt. 14:23; Luke 5:16).

Jesus modeled prayer for His disciples by publicly sharing the Lord's Prayer (Matt. 6:9-13; Luke 11:2-4). The Lord's Prayer became a model for private as well as collective times of prayer. Jesus also taught them the parable of the persistent widow so that they would not "lose heart" in their prayers (Luke 18:1-8). Jesus shares the parable of the Pharisee and the tax collector to emphasize humility and a right attitude in prayer (Luke 18:9-14). The Pharisee enters the temple full of himself, comparing himself to others, telling God how good he is. The tax collector, a typical villain in that time, enters the temple with a true sense of self-reflection and pleads for God's mercy. Jesus concludes the lesson by saying that the tax collector went home justified before God because of his humble heart and spirit.

Prayer is also waiting on God. Understanding this perspective asks us to go down the *via negativa* or negative way; that is, sometimes people learn about God by contemplating the transcendent aspects of spirituality. This is not something impossible per se, but it does ask us to contemplate the hidden aspect of God's nature. The apophatic path is very different from the worship practices and experience of most in evangelical circles. Here, a person relies more on the silent, wordless, contemplative experience rather than engaging in contemporary worship. A person relies on silence, solitude, and quiet to engage contemplative prayer that is seeking after God. If one were to observe a person only engaging in contemplative prayer, one would think that little is taking place. This way of prayer is much more than just listening. It is attentive, seeking, and responsive. It is not passive. One waits on God to do as God wills. It is not the loud call and answer of an orchestral dogfight but an attitude of slowly watching and waiting. You gradually shut off the noise and distractions around you to concentrate and focus on what the Holy Spirit has to say on a matter.

Prayer is transformed from a mechanical approach with a shopping list for God to deliver the goods and becomes a relational approach wherein we listen, pay attention, and abide with our Lord. Too often, prayer does not feel personal because we are making it into something far from God. Our prayer time should move us toward greater closeness with the Creator. As believers and followers of Jesus, we are called to participate in the Kingdom life before us. William Barclay asserts that "Eternal (*aionios*) life begins now and refers not only to length of life but also the quality of life in which we experience wholeness and union with God" (J. Johnson 2017, xviii). When we move toward prayer as waiting on God, we rely on and build our relationship with the Almighty. Consider how low and desolate King David described himself when God felt distant. Prayer enables us to stop and listen for what God has to say. It connects and empowers the believer. In prayer, we commune with God, and we know that we are not alone.

We confess that God is omnipotent, omniscient, and omnipresent. This means that we view God as all powerful, all knowing, and all present, but we do not always engage God in this manner. Christianity gives us the gift of knowing that God is always present and available. God is constantly at hand, which means we have the freedom to speak at all times and listen with no end. Jan Johnson (2017) suggests that "Contemplative prayer reveals our theology at a practical level." It shows whether our faith and our practice are balanced. It also puts us in a position wherein we learn and understand from our ever-present God. People change with a relational understanding. Johnson says, "As we surrender the common underlying belief that God has better things to do than pay attention to individual people, I begin to see that I'm not on my own" (29).

Madame Jeanne Guyon (1975) writes that "We have all been called to the depths of Christ just as surely as we have been called to salvation" (1). God has made this kind of relationship possible. It is possible through grace to all of his followers by the means of the Holy Spirit in us. Prayer is the key to experiencing Jesus in such a deep way. It is simple and holy. She suggests that prayer leads us into the presence of God as uninterrupted fellowship. This kind of prayer is not fancy, complex, or verbose. It is instead a prayer of simplicity, prayer from the heart. A person only needs to know how to seek God and pursue closeness with the Almighty. Guyon reminds us that "The Lord once promised to come and make His home within you (John 14:23). He promised to meet those who worship Him and who do His will. The Lord will meet you in your spirit" (11). She encourages us to seek God inwardly. This is where the revelations of God can be imprinted on our heart. Above all, God wants to engage us, as Guyon writes: "The Lord's chief desire is to reveal Himself to you and, in order for Him to do that, He gives you abundant grace. The Lord gives you the experience of enjoying His presence. He touches you, and His touch is so delightful that, more than even, you are drawn inwardly to Him" (13).

Fasting

Fasting is a spiritual practice found throughout scripture. A fast is abstaining from food for spiritual reasons. It is a focused time of dependence on God to sustain you. Fasting denies our flesh what it wants so that we can focus more clearly on strengthening our soul. Jesus did not fast often. In fact, his critics condemned him for "eating and drinking" (Matt. 11:19). There is only one recorded instance in scripture of Jesus fasting. This fast immediately followed His baptism (Matt. 3:13), which inaugurated Jesus' public ministry. Matthew 4:1-2 says that Jesus was led by the Holy Spirit into the wilderness to fast for forty days and nights. During that time of fasting, Jesus was repeatedly tempted by the devil. This time of testing prepared him for the next three years of ministry, but it also demonstrated that fasting can strengthen us spiritually when we use it to draw closer to God. While there is no direct command in the Bible on how to fast, we are free to use this practice as the Holy Spirit leads us. Again, the normal practice found in scripture is to abstain from food for a dedicated time. Some people fasted for one day (Judg. 20:26), one night (Dan. 6:18-24), three days (Acts 9:9), seven days (2 Sam. 12:16-23), fourteen days (Acts 27:33-34), and forty days (Deut. 9:9). Scripture shows that the length of a fast can vary, but the purpose is to draw closer to God.[12]

Worship

Jesus demonstrated worship as a spiritual practice throughout the Bible. In his humanity, Jesus is our example of how to worship. In his divinity, he is the object of our worship (Phil. 2:6). Jesus shows intentional acts of adoration, humility, submission, obedience, and praise directed toward God. During the third temptation, Jesus shows these acts of worship and reminds us that there is no substitute for our dependence on God. Jesus quotes a text from Deuteronomy and says, "Go, Satan! For it is written, 'You shall worship the Lord your God, and serve Him only'" (Matt. 4:10). The discipline of worship is a focused response toward God. Calhoun (2015) says, "Worship happens whenever we intentionally cherish God and value him above all else in life" (49). Worship can even be understood as the result of using a spiritual practice. Using the disciplines can grow our spiritual life and strengthen our relationship with the Almighty.

Worship can be seen in a broad or narrow context. Jesus conducts worship in both capacities. In the broad sense, worship is seen as a way of life (Rom. 12:1). Here, all of life can be viewed as an act of worship or service to God. Worship is also pictured as an act of the assembled people of God. This is shown in the worship prescribed by God in the tabernacle and the temple. In the tabernacle instructions, God prescribes a sacred or holy space, a sacred time – the Sabbath (Exod. 31:12-17), and His desire to dwell among the people (Exod. 25:8).

Scripture shows Jesus in worship by attending synagogue and temple assemblies (Mark 1:21-28; Luke 4:31-37; Matt. 21:23), praying (Luke 6:12), studying and teaching scripture (Luke 2:46; Luke 4:15), and bowing down to prostrate himself before God (Matt. 26:39). We also see Jesus singing a song of praise with the disciples at the conclusion of the Last Supper before going out to the Mount of Olives (Matt. 26:30; Mark 14:26). Jesus uses worship as a way to glorify the Father and maintain his relationship with the Father. Jesus shows us that God is worthy of our praise and honor. In Jesus' encounter with the Samaritan woman, he states that God is seeking true worshipers, those who worship Him in spirit and truth (John 4:21-24). In this passage, Jesus teaches that authentic worship is not based on a physical location but, rather, the location of one's heart. It is here where Jesus encourages us to build a spiritual relationship between the worshiper and God.

Spiritual practices enable us to strengthen and sustain our relationship with God. This is vital for all of humanity but especially for those contemplating suicide. When one feels helpless, hopeless, or worthless, there is incredible power in seeking God. We are reminded to place our trust in God, because he is able and strong, even though we feel weak. We can cast all of our concerns on him, as expressed in Proverbs 3:5, which says, "Trust in the Lord with all your heart. And do not lean on your own understanding." When we feel down and think that suicide might hold the answer, it is time to lean on the Lord. While we are often tempted to place faith in ourselves, it is always better to rely on the strength and power of God. We can trust in him. Spiritual exercises remind us that there is a loving and caring God who wants my fellowship. God is always available and wants to build on our relationship. Spiritual exercises remind us that we are never alone, abandoned, or forsaken. People at risk of suicide can benefit by engaging their faith and using the practices that Jesus taught his disciples. Even in the darkest moments of life, God can lift us up and provide bright hope for tomorrow. In Jesus, we find newness in life.

Spiritual Formation and Growth

The biblical picture of human life is for us to be changed by entering a relationship with Jesus and grow in that relationship. Dallas Willard explains that "We were meant to be inhabited by God and to live by a power beyond ourselves. Human problems cannot be solved by human means. Human life can never flourish unless it pulses with the 'immeasurable greatness of his power for us who believe' (Ephesians 1:19)" (2006, 17). We aim to have Jesus in us and to work by grace in tandem with him. We are called to learn and follow the ways of Jesus. Willard (2006)) says Jesus "invites us to follow him into his practices." Through long practice and by the empowerment of God's Spirit, our old bodily habits and former ways come to the side of our renewed spirit in service to God. Willard says, "The disciplines for the spiritual life are a central part of the crucial 'in-formation' which Jesus brings to us, and we dare not neglect it" (21). Slowly, gradually, and surely, we begin to look more like Jesus as we trust and model Him as our teacher. Implementing spiritual practices and disciplines in the way of Jesus "liberate[s] us into the riches of Kingdom living" and "lead[s] us into an abundance of the life that is eternal in quality and power" (38-39).

Spiritual formation is not a panacea for people considering suicide. However, growth in the spiritual disciplines helps them become stronger emotionally as well as spiritually. They focus more on God than on the reasons that cause them to despair. In moments of crisis, drastic measures need to be taken in to help people preserve their lives. In other moments, focusing on spiritual formation helps despairing people heal, gain better self-perspective, and grow in ways that protect them from suicide.

Spiritual formation is this process of growth that forms and transforms us into the way and example of Jesus. Willard refers to spiritual formation as "the process of shaping our spirit and giving it a definite character. It means the formation of our spirit in conformity with the Spirit of Christ" (2006, 53). It is the Holy Spirit at work in us creating an inward transformation. We yield and surrender more of ourselves to the way of Jesus – one in which we gradually take on the quality and character of Jesus Christ. We grow in the image of Jesus or into what is often called Christlikeness. In all of our ways, we increasingly reflect Jesus. In love, grace, and compassion, we grow into the way of God. The old self is abandoned and the new self is embraced as the path of a disciple. We become more like Jesus.

Members of the military take an oath upon entry and pledge their allegiance to the cause of freedom. They are required to be physically fit for their military mission. In the Army, soldiers are required to perform "PT" – physical training – on a routine basis. They are graded each year on the number of push-ups, sit-ups, and time it takes for them to run two miles. This form of training becomes a matter of intention, followed by formation of the physical habit to become stronger. PT allows them to stay in shape and perform their prescribed duties. Physical conditioning and strength training are not performed just to make people look good in a uniform or the mirror. The purpose of strength training is to actually use it for the daily functions of life. It is expected that everyone is physically fit for his or her role in the Armed Forces. You cannot predict when your level of strength will be necessary to save the life of a fellow soldier or yourself. Will you carry someone to safety? Can you drag someone out of harm's way? Are you able to run and deliver a message? You must be ready to respond and react should a time of crisis arise. As an Army chaplain, I see spiritual fitness and physical fitness in the same light. In order to build spiritual muscles, we must perform spiritual exercises that will make us stronger than we are today.

If people struggle with the temptation of suicide, several things can help. In addition to counseling services and other professional help that is available, people may strengthen themselves spiritually. Just as PT is important in keeping soldiers prepared in the face of harm, people susceptible to suicide can similarly prepare themselves in the face of suicidal harm. Spiritual disciplines are one way among many to aid people in despair; this is corroborated by behavioral scientific studies as well as biblical teachings. Moreover, as Christians, we believe that growing in spirituality represents growth in relationship with God. That growth is especially important as a divine means of transcendent help in times of suicidal temptation.

Spiritual practices strengthen faith. Habit formation is a critical piece to learning and building familiarity in spiritual disciplines. Athletes never lament the habits that make them better on the field. People create and perform habits to connect and grow. Spiritual practices are the critical piece of our spiritual growth. Daily and corporate practices are in our hands. God will not do these for us. Mirrors are placed in a gym so we can honestly see ourselves. The mirrors are not on the wall to make us wince but to encourage us to better health. While it may be true that many do not like the person they see in the reflection, there is always an opportunity to improve. J. P. Moreland (2019) reminds us that "Anything worth learning – playing tennis, speaking Spanish, crocheting – is awkward, unnatural, frustrating, and hard to do in the early stages of learning. You will fail repeatedly and hit the tennis ball into the net on a regular basis! But if you form the intention to stay at it, you will become better and better at what you are learning" (102). Learning, experience, and constant practice teach us how to improve.

1 Timothy 4:7-8 exhorts you to "Train yourself to be godly. For physical training is of some value, but godliness has value for all things, holding promise for both the present life and the life to come." St. Louis Cardinal Jordan Hicks threw the fastest recorded pitch in baseball history on May 20, 2018. He hurled a 105.1 mile-per-hour sinker against the Philadelphia Phillies (Gardner, 2018). That pitch moved faster than some cars can drive! Now, imagine the amount of preparation and work that must be accomplished to throw a baseball like that prior to stepping on the mound. Can anyone just pick up a baseball and throw a 105.1 mile-per-hour pitch? If you were wondering, the answer is no. Those of us watching that game saw the incredible accomplishment that he was able to

perform. Many think that the difficult work is stepping out onto the pitching mound to throw the ball. However, in reality, he was prepared for the game through an entire season of exercise, training, workouts, dieting, and practice throws. We develop spiritual muscle in the same way. Just as an athlete must spend time pumping iron, counting calories, and running on the track, we need to exercise and build spiritual muscle in a similar fashion. The spiritual practices conducted in God's gymnasium gradually become easier and sweeter, yielding a stronger individual.

Christian spiritual practices change us and our point of view. They allow us to flourish because we are spending time with God. Spiritual disciplines give peace and hope because they ultimately direct us to Jesus. Disciplines never take the place of God. Disciplines do not deliver halos from on high. Disciplines are powerful because, as Calhoun (2015) shared, they allow us to "keep company with Jesus" (19). It is during this time of communion and worship that we discover new levels of reliance and perspective. Eric Johnson (2017) suggests that reflection and spiritual practices provide a perspective that is vital to growth. He sees Christianity as therapeutic for Christians and writes that there is healing and new life when we "come to terms with our limitations and smallness before God and the universe, so that we can learn to see ourselves more from God's perspective" (207). During these moments of discovery, we realize the magnitude of God and are often humbled by our own flaws, frailty, and shortcomings. Our eyes are opened to also see how we ultimately rely on God because of our limitations, foibles, and weaknesses. Johnson notes that Balthasar called such realizations the "positivity of the finite." We are invited to come to terms with being finite creatures who have personal limitations. In our time with God, we see ourselves and others without the mask we so often hold up to impress others. Here, we find that everyone makes mistakes, that people are damaged, and that no one will ever "arrive" at a state of completion on their own. We are totally dependent on the grace and mercy of God. Time with God and involvement in spiritual practices allow us to see and know what is true. Johnson sees spiritual growth as "learning to accept one's limitations by means of resting in God and God's will for us" (208). Union with Jesus provides this peace and perspective.

With regard to those who are suicidal, there is no single solution to their questions, concerns, and despair. People are unique in what tries and tempts them. In order to help them, however, there needs to be a net of help that supports them. Among the many strings of that netting, spiritual disciplines serve an invaluable role in helping people deal with thoughts of suicide or with recovery from suicide attempts. Spiritual disciplines help people grow individually in their self-understanding and self-development; they also help people become more reliant on the gracious empowerment that God wants to instill in them. Although people may despair about being all alone and without hope, Christians believe that they are never alone. God continually abides with them, offering strength as well as guidance when they feel that all is lost.

Bodily Changes from Spiritual Practices

The Gospel of John tells us that we are born of flesh and the Spirit (John 3:6). This passage is a reminder of how the aspects of our being are closely connected with each other. Feeding our spiritual aspect can literally transform our physical body. We are still trying to fully understand how our spiritual lives interact and influence our physical ones, but the curtain is gradually being raised. When people establish a Christian life built on spiritual practices of prayer, Bible reading, and church attendance – in addition to other spiritual practices – it brings us closer to God. It also changes our bodies to better commune with Him. Our relationship with God is connected to what is happening inside us, so it can physically affect us. Rob Moll (2014) identifies how a deeper prayer life can create physical changes:

> Shorter prayers in which we make requests to God – the kind many of us are most familiar with – go undetected by a brain scan. This doesn't mean they don't work or they are not valuable. But it may encourage you toward deeper, longer prayer when you learn that twelve minutes of attentive and focused prayer every day for eight weeks changes the brain significantly enough to be measured in a brain scan. Not only that, but it strengthens areas of the brain involved in social interaction, increasing our sense of compassion and making us more sensitive to other people. It also reduces stress, bringing another measurable physical effect – lower blood pressure.

Prayer in this deeper, more attentive way also strengthens the part of the brain that helps us override our emotional and irrational urges. Prayer that seeks communion with God actually makes us more thoughtful and rational, enhances our sense of peace and well-being, and makes us more compassionate and responsive to the needs of other people. (15-16)

There is a measurable and observable difference between a brain and a brain that utilizes the spiritual practice of prayer. Researchers have identified the kind of prayer that changes our brains as the deep, focused, and attentive forms of prayer. Moll says, "Prayer that changes us involves our full concentration . . . this sort of prayer often doesn't come easily" (27). Here, Moll is referring to the use of prayer that avoids distraction. It is trying to hear the "still small voice" of God (1 Kings 19:12). Transforming prayers in this vein can be identified as the spiritual disciplines of contemplative prayer, meditation, examen, *lectio divina*, and centering prayer. Prayers and meditations call Christians to quiet their minds, remove themselves from the cares and noise of the day, and simply be in the presence of God (Moll, 28).

In neuroscience, the saying is, "Neurons that fire together wire together" (Moreland 2019). Repeated actions cause neurons to fire together, and this repetition causes certain neurons to wire together to form ingrained circuits. Like muscle memory, these circuits are habit-triggering grooves in the brain. Consider grooves like those you can see on a vinyl record or a compact disc. Both records and CDs have grooves that communicate information. A training program that eliminates bad habits and replaces them with good habits makes the body form new neural pathways. As you constantly conduct good practices, new grooves form and "change the brain's circuitry" (44). If done for two to six months, one's brain can structure and develop new grooves (67), as Moreland states:

Neuroplasticity refers to the brain's ability to form new brain grooves (i.e., new patterns of synaptic connections) and undergo a change of structure. The brain is not stuck in a static, unchanging structure. In fact, through repeated habit-forming practices of different ways of thinking, feeling, and behaving, one can reshape one's brain in a healthy direction. (67)

Continual practice makes something permanent. Repeated practice forms a new set of grooves, and these become permanent, unless one retreats to old ways.

It turns out that spirit and flesh are deeply intertwined. Our bodies are designed to engage and develop relationship with God. Moll (2014) says, "A group of neuroscientists have been studying brain systems that enable people to have spiritual experiences. As they have traced the lines of the brain in worship and meditation, these scientists have discovered that the spiritual circuit that gets exercise in prayer or in church has all kinds of positive effects" (16). Prayer slows us down to talk with and focus on God. Moll continues, "Prayer normally tends to enhance the relaxation response, which is why it reduces stress and lowers blood pressure" (23). When the spiritual brain circuit is fully engaged through exercising religious activity, we can experience a feeling of union and closeness with God, giving us a higher level of peace and joy.

Religion and spirituality seem to enhance the brain's capacity to function in several ways. Mario Beauregard says his studies confirm that "Spiritual experiences involve far more than the emotional parts of the brain, including 'a variety of functions, such as self-consciousness, emotion, body representation, visual and motor imagery, and spiritual perception" (Moll, 1998, 26). God has designed our brains with the ability to change. Andrew Newberg and Mark Robert Waldman write, "Intense, long-term contemplation of God . . . appears to permanently change the structure of those parts of the brain that control our moods, give rise to our conscious notions of self, and shape our sensory perceptions of the world." As our brains change with neurons shifting and knitting themselves together, the brain area that deals with anger becomes less active, and compassion for others grows (Moll, 26). Newberg says, "Spiritual practices enhance the neural functioning of the brain in ways that improve physical and emotional health." The more we engage our faith and use spiritual practices, we create neural pathways that strengthen us for relationships and eliminate those that detract from our growth (Moll, 27).

As Christians, we are called to live in the manner of Christ and grow in His likeness. Transformation into the image of Christ becomes possible as neurons develop new connections, as Moll (2014) describes:

> Our brains are always changing based on new experiences and new information. Neurons form new "arms" called dendrites and axons and connect to one another, making physical changes in the brain that allow us to recall a memory or information. Change doesn't come easily, but as we establish new patterns of thinking and habits, the neural pathways that were once new and difficult grow firmer and more well-traveled. (157)

The science of neuroplasticity explains how every experience changes the brain, but it also shows how the most long-lasting transformation comes by intentional and attentive training (157). This is also seen in how organizations like Alcoholics Anonymous and Narcotics Anonymous function to defeat substance abuse. The overall effectiveness of these organizations in altering substance abuse is largely attributed by researchers to their spiritual tenets and practices (Koenig 1998, 187).

Brain plasticity and the ability to learn new or better pathways in our circuitry is amazing. Gang Wu (2013) points out that "The hippocampus is one of the most plastic regions of the brain." Even though early childhood trauma, psychological stress, maltreatment, and abuse may decrease development of the hippocampus at an early age, people can still learn increased resilience instead of living in vulnerability. The main factor in determining "learned helplessness" or "resilience" is learning how to respond to stressors. When people discover that they can successfully master a mild or moderate stressor, they learn how to be resilient to a variety of later and even stronger stressors. Wu points out that "This phenomenon is called 'stress inoculation,' and occurs when the person develops an adaptive stress response and a higher-than-average resilience to negative effects of subsequent, uncontrollable stressors" (4). Stress inoculation is a form of immunity against later stressors in much the same way that vaccines induce immunity against disease.

Stress inoculation and resiliency studies are a growing body of research. Most efforts focus on how to build stronger people and develop greater coping mechanisms. The Gang Wu study reminds us that research supports the stress inoculation hypothesis and suggests that this protection may be due to neuroplasticity in the prefrontal cortex. Wu says, "Other studies have found that neural circuits involved in resilience can be modified for many years after adversity. For instance, the majority of adolescents whose development was stunted in childhood due to trauma were able to developmentally 'catch-up' when relocated to a supportive, loving environment" (2013, 4). Brain science is incredibly complex and humbling. Our bodies have been knit together in ways we are just learning to fathom. Psalm 139:14 truly says it best: we are "fearfully and wonderfully made."

It is impressive to see the connection and interplay among all of our three aspects. The outcome of using spiritual disciplines strengthens the body, mind, and spirit beyond our imagination. Perhaps we are just starting to see and understand how our bodies, minds, and spirits are truly supposed to function through God's design. Science and technology are revealing the magnificent manner of our being and the incredible mysteries of how our bodies function. We are called to change and become a new creation. Through God, learning the way of Jesus, and listening to the Holy Spirit, we change into the people of God. As we join the family and grow in faith, our bodies respond and allow us to share more of God's great love. When we take up spiritual disciplines and apply them to our life, we are physically, mentally, and spiritually transformed.

The holistic nature of who we are as people is important for understanding and ministering to those who contemplate suicide or those who are recovering from suicide attempts. Again, why people contemplate or attempt suicide is a complex issue that varies from person to person. Suicide is a giant jigsaw puzzle with a multitude of interlocking and connected parts. Religion and spirituality need to be included in the care and betterment of people who are at risk of suicide. To help them, caregivers need to embrace a variety of factors to meet the unique needs people have. If we want to give those inclined toward suicide the maximum amount of hope available, then spiritual as well as other dimensions of our humanity must be considered. Focusing on spiritual disciplines represents a significant way of helping people grow in knowledge of and relationship with God. Christians believe that growth in spiritual formation is invaluable in dealing with the worst and most despairing circumstances people face.

Spiritual Practices and Hope

It is important for us to see, feel, and understand hope. Earlier in this paper, I shared that feelings of hopelessness are one of the primary warning signs that suicidal people exhibit. Engaging religion through spiritual practices strengthens our awareness of God and provides hope. Spiritual disciplines become life-enhancing and can also be viewed as a coping resource where hope is found. Harold Koenig found that when it comes to hope, "There is both qualitative and quantitative research" showing it as an outcome of religious and spiritual practices. In the forty studies that researched the practice of religion producing hope, twenty-nine, or 73%, reported significantly positive relationships, and "no studies found an inverse relationship" (2012, 4). Hope can be found in faith. It is available to those who will seek the Lord. Using spiritual practices and spending time in our faith yield a hope that this world cannot provide.

Ellen Idler and Linda George share that "Just as individuals are prone to suicide when they are without sufficient constraint from the community, so are they vulnerable when they are lonely and isolated" (1998, 53). Hope may not feel apparent or available when we are alone. Psalm 46 declares that we are not alone, as "God is our refuge and strength, a very present help in trouble. Therefore, we will not fear, even though the earth be removed, and though the mountains be carried into the midst of the sea (1-2); The Lord of hosts is with us (7)." Using spiritual disciplines allows us to connect with God and reminds us of His constant care, guidance, and empowerment.

Hope is a protective factor against suicide. Hope can be viewed as an aspect of our spiritual well-being. Engaging our faith allows us to experience the hope that is available in the promises of God. When hope is present in our lives, it represents a huge benefit to all the aspects of our spirit, mind, and body. Stephen Post says, "Hope is the subjective sense of having a meaningful future despite obstacles . . . hope may be mediated through ritual, meditation, prayer, and traditional sacred narratives" (1998, 24). Spiritual practices often include the rituals of religion that allow us to find or receive hope in the very hour of our distress. Post also identifies prayer as a primary way to find hope.

A vast majority of people use prayer during times of trouble and conflict. People also use prayer to lift up those who are sick. Prayer allows us to engage God and remind us of His eternal protection. Religion and spiritual practices offer "coherent meaning" in the events of life and give us spiritual significance (Koenig 1998, 54). It is through these disciplines that we learn lessons and find strength to face troubles and trials. As we gain hope for today and tomorrow, religion's influence is vital because of spiritual practices.

Kaplan (2008) views hope as promoting life. He views positive psychology and biblical psychology as therapeutic ways to show people that there is a path out of their troubles. Those at risk of suicide need help to set foot on the path that gives hope. We must learn, find, and discover hope as we practice our faith. Building faith through using spiritual practices delivers hope and life. Scripture teaches a way for us to connect and learn the pathway for hope. Kaplan explains that hope frees and empowers us to discover the new life:

> Hope can free the individual from the threat of a tragic, deterministic, and suicidal view of life. Further, it offers a therapeutic alternative to a fixation on impossible choices. The quest for the heroic 'noble death' of the Greco-Roman tradition becomes irrelevant as human life becomes more hopeful and possible. This has been the great insight of the biblical tradition. (230-231)

Hope proves that our lives matter, because we matter as individuals to a loving and gracious God. This loving God pursues us and never gives up on us. God's love is unconditional; it cannot be earned or bought with our own actions. This persistent heavenly Father wants a relationship with us and wants to engage us now and for all eternity. God loves us, and we will never lose the love of God. Scripture and spiritual practices give a ringing and hopeful proclamation for us to live with hope. No matter how dark or fallen our past may have been, we can live a new life and participate in the Kingdom of God. A hope and love of this magnitude can turn the tide of suicidal behavior.

There is a growing body of scientific research that demonstrates the role religion and spirituality play in our total wellbeing. It is somewhat of a paradox, religiously speaking, to try to assess where the therapeutic help comes from: Is it from God alone? Is it from the human practice of spiritual disciplines? It is not an either/or question, of course. Instead, a great interdependence takes place between God's role and people's role in promoting the positive effects of religious beliefs and practices. Similar to Paul's words in 1 Corinthians 3:6, people are responsible for "planting" and "watering" in ways that contribute to their holistic well-being. Yet, Christians believe that God gives the "growth" that is crucial for people's coping abilities – spiritually as well as physically, emotionally, and intellectually.

So many voices, studies, papers, and journals now proclaim the positive effects of religious beliefs and practices that they can no longer be ignored. Koenig (1998) says, "The mental health influence of religious beliefs and practices – particularly when imbedded within a long-standing, well-integrated faith tradition – is largely a positive one." The time has come for vast fields of study to utilize and maximize the benefits of religion to relieve the turmoil, loneliness, and pain people experience. It is best to consider "religious beliefs and traditions that people hold are resources. These resources, then, can be used to complement and enhance the powerful psychotherapies and psychopharmacological treatments that modern medical science has now provided us" (392). Studies show that "religious involvement exhibits both preventative and therapeutic effects on mental health outcomes" (36). Religiosity and religious indicators clearly show to be coping resources, stress deterrents, and a factor in lowering depression rates and decreasing suicidal behavior (27).

Religion and spirituality can address the inner hunger all people have for connecting with the Almighty. Spiritual health is a reality for those who use and engage their faith. We have heightened wellbeing when we exercise, by God's grace, our spirit, mind, and body. When our spiritual aspect is allowed to flourish with religious beliefs, involvement, and activity, suicidal thoughts and suicidal behaviors drastically fall. The hope that religion and spirituality provide, of course, is not from ourselves but from God. The more we connect with our Creator, the more we realize how greatly we are loved, cherished, and empowered. While many outside the circle of faith may not know it or feel it, they are treasured beyond compare.

CHAPTER 5

CONGREGATIONS

The Blueprint for a Church

The church is the local expression of God's kingdom. It is formed with renewed and transformed people who follow Jesus. It is active and alive by the Holy Spirit. The Evangelical Friends Church (EFC) believes, "Those who repent of their sins and trust in Jesus Christ as their personal Savior are born again into His kingdom by His Spirit. These persons make up the true Church of Jesus Christ which is spiritual in nature and universal in scope" (EFC 2020, 11). Each believer is learning to grow and follow Jesus more closely each day. These individuals continually grow in faith as they yield more of their life to God. They desire a life that reflects God's holy standards and gracious love. They continue to grow and change so that the love of Jesus becomes a total way of life. Christianity is not just a message to be proclaimed; it is a lifestyle to be embodied. Every congregation that forms and empowers people to live in the way of Jesus can save people from suicide.

Christianity teaches that humans are alienated from God, and our needs, desires, and loves have become disordered. Eric Johnson (2017) writes, "Consequently, their greatest need is to be restored to the way of life for which they were created – but that restoration is beyond their own abilities" (19). Through faith in Christ, people learn to die to their own way, become new, and center themselves on God. Johnson also explains that "God intended the church to image the Trinitarian communion as its members help each other participate in this circle of glory, growing ever more in love with God and one another (Eph. 4:12-16), and seek in turn to draw more people into this happy communion" (36-37). Simply becoming a Christian does not end our disordered life, but it is the beginning of the end. Runners do not stop their journey once they are out of the blocks. They have more distance to travel. Accepting Jesus is the starting line in faith; it is not the finish line. In this journey, we learn the decentering of self and re-centering on Jesus. E. (2017) Johnson notes that "A merely intellectual relationship with God, based solely on conscious head knowledge is not enough to heal the unconscious regions of the soul" (66). As Christians, we are called to deepen our participation in God's glory and be transformed into the way and image of Jesus. Johnson indicates that it is God's intention for believers be ambassadors for Christ:

> Local churches serve as images of the Trinity, being sites of relational healing and strengthening in the Spirit. As Christians grow in the knowledge and love of God, they become more equipped to love, encourage, comfort, admonish, and support other Christians in the communion they share with the Father and the Son (1 John 1:3) and so contribute increasingly and reciprocally to the "growth of the body for the building up of itself in love" (Eph. 4:16). (68)

As stated earlier, the church is the local expression of God's kingdom. Renewed and transformed people accomplish this. The church or congregations can be understood as love-soaked people, a community of believers who are united by their understanding of faith and a desire to live fully in the loving example of Jesus. McKnight (2007) suggests that throughout the New Testament Paul "implores God to create vibrant communities of faith who will be swamped by the Holy Spirit and live like Spirit-prompted communities." McKnight adds that from "Genesis 12 to Revelation 22, the focus of God's redemptive work, the atoning work of God, is about the community of faith" (28). This means that the church is key to prepare people for God's kingdom work and has a redemptive purpose. We are ambassadors who function as personal representatives of God on Earth. We implore others to be reconciled to God and to the world. In this loving community, there should be a drive for congregations to constantly ask, "How can we help?", "How can we serve others?", "How can we make a difference in the life of others?" as a part of their missional praxis.

McKnight (2007) believes there should be a "desire to go out into the community rather than an overwhelming drive to have the community come to the local church" (118). To understand atonement as praxis is to understand relationship as fellowship. Wherever you go in the Bible, the work of God is to form a community in which the will of God is done, and people commune with others for the good of others. These communities are identified by love. It is not a group of individuals but a community where love redemptively creates fellowship. This is frequently seen in disenfranchised groups. Resident aliens and temporary residents are the people quick to receive and share in the love and care of the community.

Acts 11:26 shows the first time "Christian" is used in the Bible. Up until this time, following Jesus was simply known as "the Way" (Acts 9:2). In Antioch, the people look different, talk differently, and live differently from the disciples. Yet, the outward expression of love and care that they showed and exemplified in Antioch made people call them Christians. The name was not given because of what the disciples taught or believed but because they reflected the love of Jesus Christ. According to the people of Antioch, the disciples looked like Jesus. Their actions and manner of life was different. They were love-soaked people who demonstrated love as Jesus did. For someone to suggest that you resemble Jesus is quite impressive. It also means that we are living our faith correctly. The church is uniquely called to be that type of loving community – a place where love and peace flourish for everyone. Love must be seen and felt in a church. It is this outward demonstration of faith that often causes the fellowship to grow. That witness will draw people and teach others to grow in the image of Christ. McKnight (2007) writes that the "gospel itself is an ecclesial, atoning work: it works to create a community in which cracked Eikons are healed in their relationship with God, self, others, and the world" (121). God provides atonement to create a fellowship of people who love God, love others, and find healing. A gathering marked by that kind of love and compassion for others will draw people and continue to grow the family of God. Love-soaked people are the ultimate mark of a church that has been renewed and practices the Kingdom life.

Simon Peter envisions a community of faith that lives the gospel life. He explains his emphasis that they are to love one another, saying to "Honor everyone," but "Love the family of believers" (1 Pet. 2:17). "Finally, all of you, have ... love for one another" (1 Pet. 3:8), and "Above all, maintain constant love for one another, for love covers a multitude of sins" (1 Pet. 4:8). Peter's vision was for a gracious, healing, and redemptive community of fellowship.

Atonement is practicing the love of God, and this is to be the praxis for the community of Christian faith. Congregations are called to love people. That love is to be shown at all costs. Paul makes the obligation clear in Galatians 6:10, "So then, while we have opportunity, let us do good to all people, and especially to those who are of the household of the faith." Here, Paul echoes the dual goal for all Christians: love all people like neighbors and love the community of faith.

Francis Schaeffer (2006) shared that there is only one way to identify a Christian. It is clear and undeniable. It is unmistakable and easy to recognize. What is this single mark? What is this way that even outsiders will know if you follow Jesus? Schaeffer says, "Knowing that he is about to leave, Jesus prepares his disciples for what is to come. It is here that he makes clear what will be the distinguishing mark of the Christian" (14). We find it in John 13:33-35:

> Little children, I am with you a little while longer. You will seek Me; and as I said to the Jews, now I also say to you, "Where I am going, you cannot come." A new commandment I give to you, that you love one another, even as I have loved you, that you also love one another. By this all men will know that you are My disciples, if you have love for one another.

Schaeffer says, "This passage reveals the mark that Jesus gives to label a Christian not just in one era or in one locality but at all times and all places until Jesus returns" (14). Jesus does not give us a description but rather a command with a condition. Schaeffer keys in on this because, "An if is involved. If you obey, you will wear the badge Christ gave. However, since this is a command, it can be violated. The point is that it is possible to be a Christian without showing the mark, but if we expect non-Christians to know that we are Christians, we must show the mark" (15). Love is the unmistakable mark of Jesus. It is the sweet aroma that identifies us as followers of Jesus. Love declares who we are and whose we are. No one can deny those who reflect the gracious love of God. Congregations are called to love all people, all of humanity, as friends and neighbors. In the words of Jesus, we are called to "love" them as "I have loved you." In this example, churches and congregations need to respond compassionately to a hurting world. In this example, we are called to practice horizontal love, especially to those considering suicide.

The Ideal Place for Community, Care, and Fellowship

Congregations are identified in a multitude of studies and research journals as caring places where people at risk of suicide can find spiritual care, social support, integration, strength, and comfort. Religious involvement and practice have already been identified as protective factors that preserve life. Religious belief and activity are strong factors to keep people from suicide. Congregations and religious groups also function in providing support and integration. Sociologist Emile Durkheim theorized in 1897 that weak social bonds like the "lack of connectedness were among the chief causes of suicidality" (Stone 2017, 27). Durkheim argues that "Individuals who were isolated from social life, who were not active participants in families, religious groups, or community organizations, were more prone to suicide" (Koenig 1998, 52). These ideas mirror modern social network theory and consistently show support for suicide rates in the United States and abroad (53). The nineteenth-century concepts Durkheim expressed are considered scientifically valid today as social network theory. Congregations are relevant to combat suicide because they provide supportive and integrative communities. Idler and George identify how a religious group like a congregation act as a social network:

> Just as individuals are prone to suicide when they are without sufficient constraint from the community, so are they vulnerable when they are lonely and isolated. Religious groups can be thought of as social network structures to which only members have access. Membership in a religious congregation then potentially expands the number of social ties individuals have available to them. From a functional perspective, religious groups provide support and nurturance for their members; compassion and care for others is a primary teaching of all of the major world religions. In the secular world, social support is often conceptualized as either instrumental or emotional in nature, and religious congregations are potential

provider of both tangible assistance and spiritual support. (1998, 53)

Much of today's language focuses on the importance of promoting connection or connectedness. Deb Stone and her colleagues issued *Preventing Suicide: A Technical Package of Policy, Programs, and Practices* in 2017 for the National Center for Injury Prevention and Control, an agency of the Centers for Disease Control and Prevention. In this publication, Stone writes, "Connectedness is the degree to which an individual or group of individuals are socially close, interrelated, or share resources with others." The policy paper identifies multiple levels of social ecology like peers, neighbors, co-workers, families, and faith communities as ideal places for connection. She also says, "Connectedness and social capital together may protect against suicidal behavior by decreasing isolation, encouraging adaptive coping behaviors, and by increasing belongingness, personal value, and work, to help build resilience in the face of adversity" (2017, 27). Connection allows people to see and know that they are not alone. Congregations are perfectly suited to provide this reminder. Congregations can also deliver messages of love, value, importance, and self-worth for those who are down or despondent. Religious coping skills, spiritual practices, and resiliency are available to develop the spiritual aspect of our being. Communities of faith are essentially spiritual care centers located in neighborhoods across our nation. They are ready to help hurting people. Ideally, when one is hurting, the community will mobilize to meet the needs of its member and provide support. That is what love-soaked people do.

Establishing protective environments is also important for communities to address suicide. When love and concern for others turns into action, people at risk of suicide can find a stronger solution to their pain. Stone (2017) states, "The evidence suggests that creating protective environments can reduce suicide and suicide attempts and increase protective behaviors" (24). Communities that focus on people as a matter of their culture see lower rates of suicide. The policy paper specifically points out three findings to change culture in order to promote suicide prevention: 1) using a gatekeeper approach, 2) appointing assigned leaders or role models, and 3) establishing expectations for care. These factors helped to create new behaviors in the community and shift people toward action. Behaviors related to awareness of suicide risk change for the better, and the community develops greater skills and knowledge on how to respond to suicidal situations. Stone asserts that protective environment culture programs "represent a fundamental shift from viewing suicide and mental illness solely as medical problems and instead sees them as larger service-wide problems impacting the whole community" (25). A hurting person is a community concern and demands that I respond or help the individual in need.

While some may equate houses of worship to socializing with buddies on the bowling team, congregations are much more than just a social network or a place to connect. Congregations are local expressions of God's Kingdom. These communities of faith have been transformed by God and want to share the love of Jesus. Yes, people who attend religious services and integrate with congregations have larger social networks, more contacts, greater levels of support, and more resources available for care. They also receive religious education, religious coping skills, emotional support, and compassionate care. They learn spiritual practices through which to connect with God. They also have a sense of meaning and purpose that many outsiders cannot fathom. Loving parishioners who want the best for them also surround them. These love-soaked people are caring for depressed members, lonely individuals, and mental health consumers in the manner of Jesus. Congregations act to teach and build people through a biblical lens with the anticipated result of spiritual formation and growth. Congregations give more than community engagement; they introduce people to the Kingdom of God.

Strive for Something More Than Mental Ascent

Earlier in this chapter, McKnight (2007) and E. Johnson (2017) both addressed how mental ascent cannot generate the same kind of desire to live as Jesus lived and care for our neighbors. They suggested there are more steps to prepare and sustain people in their new way of life. Fostering transformation into "the way" of Jesus requires more than accepting orthodox ideas. I believe that McKnight and E. Johnson are correct. Orthodox teaching and understanding are necessary. Congregations must maintain the truth and standard of God. While teaching correct doctrine and beliefs is vital to faith, there is much more to share with people in order to create a loving and sustainable Christian community that will reflect the grace of God. Making love-soaked people requires more than merely knowing what to believe. We cannot stop there in a person's spiritual growth.

Imagine stepping into a bakery to eat a slice of homemade bread. The store smells wonderful. The aroma of fresh baked bread of wafting through the air. You can see all of the beautiful doughy creations in the glass display counter. Your mouth is watering for that first taste of warm bread to touch your tongue. You purchase the item and bite into the bread, but something is not right. It tastes bad. The slice of bread is not what you expected. It looked and smelled like the perfect loaf of bread, but the taste fell far short of what you expected. The baker only followed half of the steps on the recipe card. The right ingredients are all there, but the preparation was not followed, and now you are stuck with bread that does not taste right. Yuck!

Reducing Christianity to mental ascent is a common temptation for churches. While this puts the correct ingredients into the mixing bowl, there is more work to be done afterward. It is not the final step in the process. More is required, or else you will get a half-baked or overcooked product that no one wants. In fact, producing poor or bad bread will likely turn people away, to never visit your bakery again. Discipleship, mentoring, spiritual growth, and learning spiritual practices cannot be excluded in making a love-soaked community. They are also vital parts of the process. They cannot be ignored in the kitchen.

No, Christianity cannot be reduced to following a recipe card; rather, churches are called to make disciples who love people as Jesus does. Churches cannot omit necessary steps that shape and form people into the image of Jesus. The contemporary temptation to rely only on mental ascent is real, but it is also a poor substitute for the rich and hearty bread that must be crafted in the kitchen. Congregations must keep spiritual formation and discipleship in the recipe of developing Christians. People need encouragement and teaching that point them to be like Jesus. If we reduce Christianity to mental ascent, there is no incentive to continue moving forward in one's spiritual life or to join with the purpose of demonstrating the Kingdom of God on Earth. Conversion is meant to be the "starting line" in our Christian journey, not a "finish line."

Brian Zahnd (2016) suggests that American Christianity is getting by on a cheap substitute of what God has made available for us. We are feasting on water, when God has made something much better for us to drink. He believes that the church "has settled on a child's drink in a cardboard box with a straw, instead of the vintage wine that is marked by depth, grace, and authenticity." He advocates that a mental ascent approach holds us back from a greater and stronger Christian experience. Zahnd is concerned with congregations just getting by on a substitute or a "cotton candy Christianity" that never really satisfies what we truly need to be spiritually fed (7). We need churches that are willing to bake bread, churches and congregations who will labor and work in the kitchen to produce a sweet and savory product that draws people to Jesus. That is the original recipe and the best way to produce love-soaked people who will be caretakers in the Kingdom of God.

In Paul's letter to the Galatians, he reminds us to restore people in a spirit of gentleness as we "bear one another's burdens and thereby fulfill the law of Christ" (6:2). Paul also encourages us to "Be devoted to one another in brotherly love," to be "persevering in tribulation, devoted to prayer, contributing to the needs of the saints, practicing hospitality" (Rom. 12:10, 12-13). These are key components that cannot be overlooked. Paul is telling us to keep these items on the recipe card for growing people. He is telling us how to bake bread. Christianity is not just a message to be proclaimed; it is a lifestyle to be embodied. Christianity is more than knowing there is a God; it is living like God desires. We are called to demonstrate and practice the Kingdom of God here and now.

Community life is incredibly important at all levels of faith. We need the strength and safety it provides. We need the teaching elements to learn, grow, and give. We also need the community to help us during tough days. Bonhoeffer (1993) reminds us that most of our day will likely be in an unchristian environment, a place where we may be the only light shining for God. We will be outside the safety of the church walls and the protection of the community. This will be the time of our testing. Here is the place that will show our own capacity to be like Jesus. These moments and adventures outside the fellowship are the truest test of our time in Christian meditation and community. Will it yield fruit or create a leafy tree that provides shade and no sustenance? Has the fellowship served to make the individual believer strong and mature or weak and dependent? Bonhoeffer identifies this as "one of the most searching and critical questions that can be put to any Christian fellowship" (88). It essentially shows if there has been an encounter with God where the believer emerges strengthened, changed, transformed, and renewed. Did the spiritual disciplines from early in the day deliver a short burst of strength, or did it make the Word of God lodge deep inside, compelling the believer to love and obedience? Only the day can decide. Only time outside of the church walls can tell. Whatever the result, it tells the story of the fellowship, and the Christian community will feel its effects.

There is a great hunger for community. As people seek relational support in a congregation, they likely have several misconceptions of what fellowship and community are. Community is not a consumer item. It is not a luxury that can be purchased at a retreat, club, gym, spa, or church. Community is not a commodity; it emerges from our common struggle to follow in the way of Christ. The church is an alternative community, an alternative to human communities that live by force, coercion, competition, and self-interest; the church is a people that practice the holy otherness of God. Congregations like this serve as a sharp contrast to the world. David Augsburger (2006) writes, "Community is the natural setting for healing, and in positive community, persons are sustained and guided, sometimes confronted and corrected, always accepted and prized. In negative community, injured persons may be bypassed; oppressed persons often become invisible" (77). Augsburger believes that the highest word for love in the Bible "is not agape, but koinonia, the mutual, reciprocal, committed, and celebrated love of intimate relationship, authentic community, and responsive fellowship" (69). When congregations provide such a community, they offer a first-century discipleship model that puts attractional models to shame.

There is a hunger for true and authentic community, one that reflects caring and committed relationships built on the vertical love of God and horizontal love of neighbor. Our world offers many substitutes, but they all fall short. Churches cannot fall into the temptation of offering a substitute for community instead of the real deal. Congregations must offer Koinonia, the kind of fellowship that produces love-soaked people whom can be found only in a gathering of people devoted to the way of Jesus. These churches and congregations have a vital role in suicide prevention. They can offer fellowship and friendship to those who are alone and hurting. They can gather and build connection. They can teach people about the rich love of God and allow our suffering brothers and sisters to see how much God loves them. Such congregations must take up the challenge to go against the grain of our current attractional church culture, continue to care for others, and teach the loving example of Jesus.

God cares about people. Jesus bled, died, and rose again for people. The Holy Spirit is drawing the church to help hurting and broken people who desperately need a shepherd. Transformed and renewed people make up the church. These people have accepted a different way of life, one that is counter to the world. The world's economy is ruled by money, power, and control. God's economy is different: by losing your life you find it, by giving you receive, by serving you are served, by humbling yourself you are exalted. Jesus emptied himself to save the broken-hearted. We need congregations who will continue in the way of Jesus Christ. The church is how God wants to demonstrate his love for each soul he created. If we can pivot to back to baking good bread, congregations can return to their divinely-appointed task and purpose. There are suicidal people waiting for us to pivot and provide the love our world seems to have lost.

What to Teach and Offer

This section specifically addresses ministry applications and lessons that can move congregations and Christian leaders forward to help people at risk of suicide. Conditions are ripe for Christian communities to engage this hurting population, but to do so, changes need to be made in many critical areas. The overarching theme is that congregations must build people in the image of Jesus. Congregations must have love-soaked people on the frontline of engaging neighborhoods and communities. These seven steps will enable churches to rescue the perishing and stop the silence surrounding suicide.

Step One: Congregations Must Be Loving

Francis Schaeffer (2006) wrote that love is the mark of a Christian. He shows that John's Gospel declares a new and incredible commandment from Christ, "that you love one another, even as I have loved you" (13:33-35). We are to show the unconditional love and grace of Jesus. Christianity can be reduced to practically nothing, but people will know you are a Christian if you love people as Jesus. Schaeffer writes, "Love – and the unity it attests to – is the mark Christ gave Christians to wear before the world. Only with this mark may the world know that Christians are indeed Christians and that Jesus was sent by the Father" (59). People at risk of suicide need to see, feel, and experience this kind of love when they approach congregations and Christian leaders. They cannot be seen as a consumer of goods or entertainment. People at risk of suicide must be viewed as fellow travelers who need a relationship with Jesus, as equals instead of people sick with a mental illness. These men and women must be loved and respected because it is in our inner being, our way of reflecting the righteousness of God. Too often, people with mental health issues are ridiculed or rejected. They often need a place and a people for support, fellowship, and community. They are isolated, alone, and struggling. Churches that resemble families more than businesses can provide safe harbor, support, fellowship, community, and friendship. Congregations are the perfect support system for someone who needs a trusted friend during a difficult time.

Congregations are also a safe place to feel and know the love of God. They must be at the forefront of demonstrating love, acceptance, and support. Consider the needs of mental health consumers: if the church offers a cold shoulder to this group of people, then it prevents a loving response to people who need help. Amy Simpson (2013) warns that if this happens, "We have taken our cue from the world around us and ignored, marginalized, and laughed at the mentally ill" (19). This is not the love or care that Jesus would provide. Hurting people want to know that they are not alone. Simpson explains that "People desperately need to experience the love and empathy of their fellow human beings and to know that their Creator has not abandoned them" (16). The church cannot be a place where nothing is done to help. It is the physical expression of Jesus on Earth. Our healthcare system does not give what the congregations can and must provide. Churches must stand as a beacon of compassionate care and loving fellowship where all are welcome to enter.

It should be no surprise that congregations and church leaders are highly sought after in the matter of suicide prevention. They offer love and grace to people who often find it nowhere else. The American Psychiatric Association Foundation (APAF) points out why congregations and clergy are vital to providing a community approach. They are unique in what they have to offer hurting people. The APAF states that "Faith leaders encounter individuals with mental health conditions in a number of circumstances that require different approaches. They are always called to see the person rather than the illness first, and to understand their own religious assumptions regarding the role of the divine in their encounters with others" (2016). We are called to be different from the clinician who sees an illness. We are called to see the person. I am reminded of Mark 1:40-45, the passage where a leper comes to Jesus. It is hard to imagine being the leper, being viewed with disdain and disgust all of your life – being an outcast. People turn away from you and keep their kids from you. Some believe you are cursed by God. Now you come face to face with Jesus. He does not run away. Jesus stops and talks with you. He looks into your eyes and sees you. Then, he touches you. For the first time in years, someone has cared enough to see, talk to, and touch you. While the leper is cleansed with an incredible miracle, we too can heal people just by seeing them and inviting them into a place of fellowship. That is what the church is called to be. Community and fellowship from congregations can stop suicide.

Step Two: Churches Must Be a Faithful Presence

Worship opportunities and teaching are a part of what churches can offer communities. Coming together around the message of Jesus is vital to strengthening our faith. We all need reminders of faith, hope, and love during dark and troubling times. When people engage their faith, suicide rates decrease. Religiosity is a deterrent to suicide, suicidal behavior, and suicidal ideation. Multiple studies mentioned in chapter four show how religious involvement lowers the risk of suicide.[13] Andrew Wu and his colleagues showed a 71% protective benefit of religion and spirituality within Western traditions (2015, 1). There is no protective factor identified by the clinical sciences in scope or scale that compares to the protective benefits of religion and spirituality against suicide. If churches will continue to provide worship, make time for prayer, teach scripture, and share the sacraments, they will provide the strongest benefit known to counter suicide.

In scripture, we find congregations sharing the message of Jesus, mentoring people as disciples, supporting each other through prayer, practicing fellowship and community with believers, and caring for the needs of the poor. People of faith move to act and care for one another. Hunter (2010) writes that we need to recapture a theology of faithful presence, one that is also viewed as engagement in and with the world around us. Hunter describes this presence:

> First, faithful presence means that we are to be fully present to each other within the community of faith and fully present to those who are not. Whether within the community of believers or among those outside the church, we imitate our creator and redeemer; we pursue each other, identify with each other, and direct our lives toward the flourishing of each other through sacrificial love. (244)

This seems to suggest that a healthy church has nothing to do with the actual number of congregants. Instead, it focuses on how well the people are shaped and transformed into the image of Christ. Are they saturated with the love of Jesus? Do love and kindness radiate through them? Would a stranger say that they look like Jesus? Just as trees are known by the fruit they produce; Christians should also be marked by their conduct. What do they reflect? Is it the example of our secular world or the example of Jesus? Congregations must be able to extend grace through faithful presence in both arenas. Scripture makes it clear that a faithful presence is required in and outside of the fellowship. In the laws outlining holiness and human witness, scripture proclaims that "When a stranger resides with you in your land, you shall do him no wrong. The stranger who resides with you shall be to you as the native among you, and you shall love him as yourself, for you were aliens in the land of Egypt: I am the Lord your God" (Lev. 19:33-34). In Hunter's words, "To welcome the stranger – those outside of the community of faith – is to welcome Christ. Believer or nonbeliever, attractive or unattractive, admirable or disreputable, upstanding or vile – the stranger is marked by the image of God" (2010, 245). This means seeing people as equals and sharing fellowship with them in spite of any reservations we may hold. When a congregation is able to bear fruit such as this, Christians and strangers alike will be able to identify the loving and faithful presence of God, no matter the size of the church.

Step Three: Congregations Must Provide Community and Fellowship

There is no wireless substitute for a hug, handshake, or warm conversation. These simple forms of affection can be visceral reminders to people that they are loved and they matter. Bonhoeffer (1993) reminds us that the "physical presence of other Christians is a source of incomparable joy and strength to the believer" (19). Community is powerful because it is more than just a handshake; it is an expression of Christian love. Bonhoeffer states that "Christianity means community through Jesus Christ and in Jesus Christ" (21). Congregations are the gathering and the embodiment of Christ's Kingdom on Earth. They are a reflection of God's great love, as expressed by Bonhoeffer:

> The prisoner, the sick person, the Christian in exile sees in the companionship of a fellow Christian a physical sign of the gracious presence of the triune God. Visitor and visited in loneliness recognize in each other the Christ who is present in the body; they receive and meet each other as one meets the Lord, in reverence, humility, and joy. (20)

Community is a vital connection for congregations to provide those at risk of suicide. Karen Mason (2014) reminds us that "Church attendance protects against suicide." Attending worship services and Bible studies does more than merely provide social support. It offers a spiritual component that the connectedness and social support fail to register. The religious events are much more than just belonging to a civic organization, social club, or a gym. Practicing your faith in a community promotes "self-regulation and self-control" (179). People who practice their faith "rein in socially non-normative behavior and promote socially normative behavior" (180).

Culture and connectedness take their place, establishing what the community norms should look like. Church is a place to be, connect, and practice the lessons of faith. It is where all who attend can focus on holy living. Suicidal people need to practice these lessons, also. This is how they build strength and spiritual formation, as well.

In a meta-analytic study of 2,339 completed suicides and 5,252 matched controls, Andrew Wu and his colleagues showed a 71% protective benefit of religion and spirituality within Western traditions and 81% when further religion and spirituality is shared in a community (2015, 1). When faith is engaged in community, the protective benefit against suicide goes up an additional ten percent. Community and fellowship within a congregation can save lives and strengthen the people who participate in it. Congregations are identified in a multitude of studies and research journals as caring places where people at risk of suicide can find spiritual care, social support, integration, strength, and comfort. Connection in the community of faith allows people to see and know that they are not alone. Congregations are perfectly suited to provide this reminder to hurting people, delivering messages of love, value, importance, and self-worth for those who are down or despondent.

Step Four: Churches Must Practice the Priesthood of All Believers

Leaders need to equip and enable others to use their gifts for ministry. Every Christian has a role within the body of the church. God enables everyone for a work, task, or purpose. People must not be merely consumers of Christianity; they must engage their faith. We all have a God-given gift or ability to use in advancing the Kingdom of God. Some have gifts to equip the church and build it up. Others have gifts to be the church. All of these gifts were given to us so that we might be united in becoming like Jesus and living as embodiments of the Kingdom of God. The same can be said for suicide prevention efforts within a congregation. There are spiritual roles – leadership roles, facilitator roles, visitation roles, and participation roles – that can accommodate the needs of suffering people.

John Wesley gave people roles and responsibilities with the Methodist movement. Henderson (2016) explains: "Although Martin Luther had boldly proclaimed the 'priesthood of all believers' in the sixteenth century, that ideal had never become a reality even in the Protestant Church. Wesley however mobilized the entire Methodist membership that nearly every member had some share in the ministry of the congregation." (138) Henderson points out that this sharing of leadership and education roles "called for a totally different approach to spiritual and educational leadership. Rather than performing the 'ministry' themselves, the leaders' main task was the training or equipping of the leaders at lower levels" (138). We find this in scripture when Paul instructed the church at Ephesus about the fivefold gifts for ministry: "And He gave some as apostles, and some as prophets, and some as evangelists, and some as pastors and teachers, for the equipping of the saints for the work of service, to the building up of the body of Christ" (Eph. 4:11-12). These gifts, along with others described in scripture, open up a space where people become interdependent, and the Holy Spirit works in that interdependence. Instead of the striving, competition, and rancor of our secular world, a community is formed by the mutual participation in the presence of God, who is at the core. If the church used this principle more fully, then no doubt there would be less burn out and pastoral turnover in our congregations. Leaders who do not practice the priesthood of all believers practice a one-person ministry. This is extremely limited in scope and makes one weary. We should not be threatened by such a sharing of ministerial function; rather, we should be glad that believers have a direct role in shaping the next generation of disciples.

Another important distinction in engaging this lesson is that a congregation of any size can utilize it. Under the priesthood formula, you train and equip people to use their gifts and talents. Congregations focus on what they can do for mental health consumers and people with thoughts of suicide. Although some people argue that only large churches are successful because of their size, in fact, all churches can make an eternal impact in caring for people. There is no effort too big or too small. You can train the church or be the church. Both are important and very necessary for assisting others. Any attempt to engage those who suffer is a righteous effort.

If a congregation appointed one or two people to conduct hospital visits for mental health consumers and people with thoughts of suicide, it would create a huge support function for hurting people. Responding to a mental health crisis the same way the congregation responds to any other health crisis shows a level of compassion many churches avoid. It shows that the church is willing to accompany mental health consumers and at-risk individuals in their suffering without trying to fix them. Presence alone holds tremendous power. If church members can show up when it is uncomfortable or scary, then they stand as a reminder that God will not abandon those in pain. Visitations without judgment are powerful demonstrations of lovingkindness. Keefe (2018) points out that conversation and hospital visits "illustrate that Jesus is more likely to offer forgiveness and compassion than judgment and punishment [which] might be what someone needs to change their understanding of who God is" (23). We all have something to offer and contribute in an effort to grow the Kingdom of God.

Step Five: Congregations Must Teach Spiritual Formation

Congregations and leaders must emphasize ways to build spiritual growth in people. This is how we form obedient followers of Christ. The church betrays itself, the world, and our Lord if it does not provide a thorough way to build spiritual formation through Christ. Willard highlights using and putting "time-tested, biblical disciplines for the spiritual life into sensible practice [as it] will soon lead us into an abundance of the life that is eternal in quality and power" (2006, 39). He sees spiritual formation as "the process of shaping our spirit and giving it a definite character. It means the formation of our spirit in conformity with the Spirit of Christ" (53). Discipleship, disciplines, and spiritual formation change us from the professing Christian to the obedient follower. Willard believes that this is a "whole life process dealing with change in every essential part of the person" (55). As we learn to trust and obey the way of God, we gradually take on the quality, character, and manner of Jesus, having learned to respond to the leading of the Holy Spirit.

Wesley's method emphasized the importance of undertaking more than a simple sermon each week to become an obedient disciple. Small group meetings and accountability were vital to increase spiritual formation. Growth can be fashioned this way, but we often need more training to turn holy habits into routine demonstrations of faith. Wesley found a way to teach in a small group setting through classes and bands. You had to be in a class meeting in order to participate in the larger society or local congregation. The classes and bands provided an intimate place for relationships and community to develop, but they also stressed the use of spiritual practices to build holiness. Bands especially focused on confession, prayer, study, and self-examination. Henderson (2016) says, "The central function of the band methodology was what Wesley termed 'close conversation,' by which he meant soul searching examination, not so much of behavior and ideas, but of motives and heartfelt impressions" (112-113). We need more than a weekly sermon to sustain people in the way of Christ.

The desire to know and love God fuels spiritual exercises. Calhoun (2015) says that "From its beginning the church linked the desire for more of God to intentional practices, relationships and experiences that gave people space in their lives to 'keep company' with Jesus. These intentional practices, relationships and exercises we know as spiritual disciplines." The Book of Acts outlines the disciples utilizing spiritual exercises of compassion, intercession, service, prayer, fasting, and discernment (19). Seeing the disciplines as a way to keep company with Jesus is a helpful path through which to grow and develop our relationship and connection with God.

Spiritual exercises can take many forms. Calhoun (2015) identifies over seventy practices that can be considered spiritual formation in *Spiritual Disciplines Handbook* (12-16). Calhoun provides a section entitled, "Share my life with others" that specifically focuses on supporting people. The disciplines of community, connection, covenant group, discipling, hospitality, mentoring, service, small group, and spiritual friendship are just a few that she lists (7-8). All of these spiritual disciplines can strengthen people by sharing a part of your life with others. Spiritual exercises can also involve joining with another person to discuss spiritual matters or life issues. Finding a spiritual friend or mentor could go a long way toward ending isolation and loneliness for many suicidal people. It could also be finding support and knowing that your congregation has resources and groups to join. Suicide is a complex jigsaw puzzle with multiple parts and pieces. Encouraging involvement in religious activities strengthens people's reasons for living, giving at-risk people a place to belong and serve, teaching them how to foster their relationship in God's everlasting love (Mason 2014, 39). Increasing their interaction with spiritual practices builds the protective factors necessary to strengthen their faith and thwart times of self-doubt. Calhoun adds that by "Interacting with others we learn the vulnerability of giving and receiving love.... By appropriately opening ourselves to each other in the presence of Christ we discover ways to 'lay down our lives for our friends.' We learn how to become safe people who bring God's welcoming embrace to others" (2015, 141). Engaging spiritual practices allows everyone to feel the welcoming embrace of God.

Spiritual disciplines are important to helping people at risk of suicide. Mason reminds us, "Studies have found that religiosity protects against suicide" (2014, 17-18). When people practice their faith, they rely on it as a protective factor that can keep them from suicidal behavior. Protective factors can be visualized as a dam that holds back the tremendous stress and strain of a reservoir. Religion and spiritual practices can help people endure the suicidal waters on the other side of the dam. Among adults, protective factors include support by family, friends, and spouses; church attendance; prayer; worshipping God; meditation; reading scripture; and meeting with a spiritual leader (38). Studies take this step even farther. Clinical epidemiology shows religious and spiritual engagement to be the leading protective factor conferring prevention against suicide. In a meta-analytic study of over 2,000 cases of completed suicide and 5,000 matched controls, Wu and colleagues showed a 71% protective benefit of religion and spirituality within Western traditions and 81% when further religion and spirituality is shared in a community (2015, 1). Religion is not just a protective factor but also the strongest protective factor against suicide. This means that religion and spirituality show a higher protective factor against suicide than healthcare, medical prescriptions, and treatment. Of course, as Christians, we believe that God graciously aids us as we minister to one another, including those contemplating suicide.

Spiritual exercises help people connect with Christ. Lund (2014) says that "Turning to spiritual practices such as prayer and meditation can help bring comfort and a sense of inner peace during times of suffering" (81). Spiritual practices vary, but they all carry the power to redeem and strengthen our soul. These practices build and transform us in vital ways. We receive spiritual growth and build the spiritual muscle necessary for difficult days. In the praxis of our faith, we learn how to become like Jesus. Congregations and Christian leaders can address the issue of suicide by returning to a scriptural blueprint of disciple-making and forming people into the image of Christ.

Step Six: Congregations Must Reduce Stigma

Both word and deed can reduce stigma. Churches must talk about suicide and act to help those with thoughts of suicide. Churches would do an incredible amount of good by accepting the physical, mental, and spiritual aspects of our humanity to address suicide. As mentioned in the first chapter, churches cannot totally yield their helping spiritual role to science and medicine. Likewise, churches cannot totally exclude medical methods and suggest that suicide is strictly a spiritual matter. This smacks of Gnosticism in caring for people and ignores the physical realities of how we are created. Churches need to embrace the physical, mental, and spiritual aspects of how God made us. At the end of the age, God will not ask how many people felt comfortable by attending a local congregation. God will ask, "Did you care for my sheep?"

Ending stigma requires congregations to practice love. Lund (2014) reminds everyone that "Life is filled with diseases that cause us pain and suffering.... Mental illness is a biochemical reality, like cancer, and heart disease, and all the things we wish would go away" (83). This is part of the human story, and in it there is a role for congregations to share the love of God. None of us is perfect, and so we should not demand perfection of those who enter through the church doors. As image bearers, we are called to represent the Kingdom of God and express the holy love and example of Jesus. Scripture commands us to love and care for our brothers and sisters. There is qualification in these passages. Congregations are called to love one another, in spite of weaknesses, imperfections, and peculiarities. As followers of Jesus, our love should continually increase. Christian examples of charity and compassion should flow out of us. Love should grow within us in both scope and depth. "Yet," Lund warns, "too often Christian communities cause more harm and suffering by suggesting that mental illness is something shameful and somehow a sign of unfaithfulness and even sinfulness" (83). The fellowship of God often fears, distrusts, and even marginalizes mental health consumers and their families. It is a tragedy when faith communities push shame and stigma, instead of healing and reconciliation, onto wounded people. Congregations must not behave or communicate in ways that would shame, frighten, or reject mental health consumers. If they do, then the church's actions create stigma and even more suffering for someone who needs our care. Lund outlines how this occurs:

> When mental illness is viewed strictly as a spiritual disease and not a brain disease, God is often viewed as the one in charge of administering mental illness as a punishment. Viewing mental illness only as a spiritual disease contributes to the stigma and shame of people who suffer from mental illness. It is tragic that Christian communities, the very communities in which sufferers seek compassion, acceptance, understanding, healing, and love can be the communities that inflict the most harm. (85)

Stigma is real. It pushes people away from church and from God. Congregations can turn that tide by fighting a wrong attitude and teaching that there is a place for both scientific and spiritual solutions. Congregations need to push back on any appearance of rejection or shame. If a person is already contemplating suicide, then less than loving attitudes might push that person into even greater darkness. Stigma must stop within church communities because it goes against the grain of God. Lund (2014) emphasizes that there is a better way, saying, "As Christians we recall Jesus' way of blessing those who are marginalized: the sick, the hungry, the poor, the imprisoned. Jesus blesses people who have mental illness, extending divine love, grace, and spiritual healing. Blessed are the crazy for we shall be called children of God" (98).

Consider the powerful impact of visiting someone at risk of suicide during or after a hospitalization. On this matter, the National Action Alliance for Suicide Prevention states the following:

> The transition from inpatient to outpatient behavioral health care is a critical time for patients with a history of suicide risk and for the health care systems and providers who serve them. In the month after patients leave inpatient psychiatric care, their suicide death rate

is 300 times higher (in the first week) and 200 times higher (in the first month) than the general population's (Chung et al., 2019). Their suicide risk remains high for up to three months after discharge (Olfson et al., 2016; Walter et al., 2019) and for some, their elevated risk endures after discharge. (2019, 1)

This is a critical time in which congregations should show love for and be present with someone who does not value their own life. Congregations likely have mental health consumers as members or attendees and should make an effort to conduct in-person visits once a suicidal individual is discharged. As well, congregations should make hospital visits to mental health centers and behavioral health clinics. They should coordinate a visit or send caring contacts to a person during the first twenty-four hours after being discharged. This moment of crisis needs the church to rise up and support the soul who cannot imagine another sunrise. With suicide rates elevated to 300 and 200 times the norm, we must move beyond the silence of stigma and run toward action. I fully recognize that this may present difficult and delicate situations that are not easy to handle. It would take a persistent and diligent friend to wade through the awkward and uncomfortable stigma associated with inpatient and outpatient visitations, but the simple act of a short hospital visit just might save a life. Just as Paul called out to stop the Philippian jailer from plunging a sword into his chest, so we must speak out and act to preserve the life of hurting people. We cannot afford to remain silent regarding suicide.

In 1 Corinthians 12, Paul reminds us that the church is one body made up of many different members. Keefe (2018) believes, "The beauty of this is that the stronger members are charged with caring for the weaker, more vulnerable members." Jesus challenged people with power to throw stones only if they had no sin. Many must hear the reminder of Jesus before they will drop the rocks from their clenched fists. Keefe affirms that "Individually, we all sin, we all hurt, we all fall short. However, when we come together, Christ commands us to care for those among us who are the most vulnerable" (2018, 31). Consider how many people have been turned away from church. Each time this happens, it implies that someone is unworthy, unwanted, and unloved. This does not embody Jesus. The gathered community of Christ has a responsibility to close ranks with the broken and battered people around us. We are called to love people who see only darkness and despair. We are called to provide compassionate care just as the Good Samaritan did. We cannot leave someone broken, battered, and alone on the side streets where we live. Keefe says, "This is church at its best. When church can set aside issues of budget, building, and butts in the pews – all its fears – to care for those who are most vulnerable, then church is what it was meant to be, namely, lifesaving" (31). Congregations must reduce stigma by seeking out those who are on the margins of existence and offer them a place of healing, comfort, and care.

Churches can also reduce stigma by teaching members to practice self-awareness and attitudinal neutrality. We all have an opinion when it comes to the topic of suicide. The challenge of our day, however, is to hold our own thoughts in check, especially if they might harm someone who is contemplating suicide. Practicing self-awareness and attitudinal neutrality creates ready, willing, and able caregivers who will respond to people at risk of suicide. A foundational understanding for caregivers is the necessity of attitudinal neutrality. We need to understand our own attitudes and opinions regarding suicide before we can truly help others in need. Ramsay writes, "Self-knowledge helps us set aside those things within us that may hinder helping relationships and make it difficult for us to attend to the needs of a person at risk" (2004, 7). Self-knowledge allows us to reflect and wrestle with the subject before we start helping others. Instead of wearing an opinion on your sleeve, consider the power of being a neutral presence when someone wants to talk about the difficult subject of suicide. When we practice attitudinal neutrality, we allow conversations and relationships to be formed even around the most difficult subjects. Discussing the topic of suicide would certainly qualify for that moniker. It is okay to disagree with someone who reveals a desire to die by suicide. The challenge is to hold your opinion and focus your attention on helping the at-risk person choose life or seek community resources. Being neutral is very difficult, but it yields an incredible reward to those suffering with thoughts of suicide. It also demonstrates love and respect for the individual. Neutrality essentially cancels stigma. You do not show your cards. You do not express your opinion. You only focus on being present and building a relationship with someone who needs to know the love of God.

Step Seven: Churches Should Embrace Gatekeeping

Many people in distress do not seek help or support on their own. Identifying people at risk of suicide can help to reach those in the greatest need and connect them to immediate care and support. Although screening and assessing patients for suicide risk is becoming more common in health care settings, many people at risk of suicide do not seek health care professionals in the critical weeks, days, or hours before they harm themselves. However, they more likely seek out clergy or church leaders for immediate help. Congregations can help those at risk of suicide by knowing how to recognize and respond to different warning signs. Utilizing gatekeepers in a church can reduce suicide and point at-risk people to resources during a time of personal crisis.

Congregations can address suicide with knowledge and care for those who need help. Knowing the signs of suicide is vitally important. It allows a community to provide help for those in pain. Ramsay (2004) points out that "A sudden, painful event may set off or hasten a decision to die by suicide, but it is unlikely to be the only cause. More typically, other contributing events and feelings have occurred over a prolonged period of time" (22). Suicide can be addressed where we live. With help, human beings are capable of withstanding almost any kind of loss, turmoil, or suffering; therefore, we cannot avoid discussions about suicide. Addressing such uncomfortable topics is exactly what caring people should do. Our silence on the subject may be fatal.

Suicidal circumstances are not difficult to understand. We are able to realize when people are happy, and we are also able to realize when people are in pain. Suicides are often telegraphed, as Ramsay (2014) explains: "Most people communicate how they are reacting to or feeling about the events that are drawing them toward suicide. These communications – or invitations for others to offer help – come in the form of direct statements, physical signs, emotional reactions, or behavioral cues" (23). People with suicidal thoughts normally share that suicide might be under consideration. Those at risk normally give warnings, but communities too often miss the invitations and cries for help.

Education is vital to recognizing the warning signs of suicide, whereas ignorance can prove to be fatal for those around us.

Gatekeeping is listed as a national best practice to reduce suicide. According to the U.S. Department of Health and Human Services Office of the Surgeon General and National Action Alliance for Suicide Prevention (HHS), gatekeeping is documented as a community best practice within the National Strategy for Suicide Prevention (2012) under several goals and objectives (56, 72, 126, 128). It is commonly used in educational, healthcare, medical, and military settings for suicide prevention (Burnette 2015, 2). Burnette identifies gatekeeping as a suicide prevention model that teaches how to "identify individuals who may be at risk of suicide, provide immediate support, and refer them to an appropriate individual who is able to offer help" (1). This model relies on individual gatekeepers to monitor people for the signs and symptoms of suicide. Burnette describes them as "individuals in a community who have face-to-face contact with large numbers of community members as part of their usual routine" (2). Most adults and adolescents can be trained as gatekeepers; it just takes time to select and train individual gatekeepers. Gatekeeping community models require agencies and organizations to pick a suicide prevention course or program to teach gatekeepers. Gatekeeper programs typically discuss education on suicide, common attitudes, beliefs, and opinions regarding suicide, how to identify warning signs, listening to people with thoughts of suicide, and referring them to a caring individual. The Suicide Prevention Resource Center (SPRC) identifies twenty-eight different gatekeeper programs available to use (2020, 2-17). All of these programs can be tailored and adjusted to specific groups. The SPRC states, "Specific audiences for gatekeeper training include those who have regular contact with people who may be at increased risk for suicide, such as high school teachers and students; first responders; faith community leaders; and people who work with older adults" (2018, 1). All gatekeeper trainings teach the same concepts, but they often differ in their complexity, length, format, and target audience (2020, 1-2).

Burnette states, "There is substantial evidence that training can increase both declarative and perceived knowledge about suicide. Those who receive gatekeeper training are generally better able to recognize warning signs of suicide and choose effective intervention strategies compared with those who have not received training" (2015, 5-6). This is a significant reason why churches should adopt a gatekeeper model for leadership, staff, teachers, volunteers, and employees. If congregations utilize love-soaked members to approach those hurting with thoughts of suicide, then moments of crises can be averted or treated by caring people on site. Christians who are dedicated to tailoring their life after Jesus are the perfect people to serve as gatekeepers. They care for the marginalized in any setting. They want to help the hopeless and alleviate their pain and suffering because they love God and their neighbor. Gatekeeping can serve as a simple way to make churches approachable, share true fellowship with others, and offer the welcoming love of God to spiritually injured people. Gatekeepers do not need to be therapists, counselors, or clinicians, and they do not need to solve the problem or issues that suicide presents. They only need to know the signs of suicide, ask those who exhibit such signs, and connect them to a caring resource for help. In this way, they can learn how to help people who suffer with the psychache of suicide. Gatekeeping is similar to learning CPR or cardio pulmonary resuscitation. You focus on keeping the person at risk of suicide alive until you can hand the individual off to a caring professional or a local resource. This intervention technique often is called suicide first aid. Nearly any adult or teen can learn the skills to become a gatekeeper.

While there is a great benefit to training gatekeepers, there are limits to gatekeeper community models. There is limited research and evidence to show that training develops more adaptive or desirable attitudes about suicide prevention. Gatekeepers acquire the knowledge and learn how to provide help for suicidal people, but the training may not change the gatekeeper's beliefs. The training does not necessarily transform them to think and behave like new people. They may continue to hold negative attitudes about suicidal people, refuse to intervene, or avoid the topic altogether. Burnette (2015) points out that "Potential gatekeepers may be reluctant or unlikely to intervene with an at-risk individual because they feel that it is not their responsibility or that it is inappropriate to intervene. The stigma of mental illness is one reason for gatekeeper reluctance" (8), because he most common response to this stigma is to avoid those believed to have a mental illness.

The church can address avoidance and stigma better than most social support structures. Churches are the perfect place to find and use gatekeepers because of their commitment to be loving and gracious people. Avoidance could be a fear of discussing depression and suicide while in conversation with at-risk individuals. Burnette says it could also be the concern of "attributing the label of mental illness to another individual, which they fear could cause further distress" (2015, 9). Fear and avoidance cannot be accepted in a gatekeeper's role, as these behaviors can prove fatal. Potential gatekeepers may not feel comfortable interacting with people in distress or suicidal crisis, which is why randomly selecting a person to become a suicide prevention gatekeeper in any community is a problem and is likely the weak link in the chain of many gatekeeper programs. Many agencies and organizations who use gatekeepers do not vet those who are trained as gatekeepers. You must have the right type of person for the job, or else it becomes meaningless. Forcing someone to become a gatekeeper or attend gatekeeper training to increase institutional metrics is a false solution. Just because you have more certified gatekeepers in a school, healthcare facility, army post, or college campus does not guarantee a reduction in suicidal activity. Gatekeeping requires a mature and caring individual who will intervene and engage people who hold potential thoughts of suicide. Gatekeeper training does not transform people into compassionate souls; that is the role of the church. This is why it is so important to select and train mature and loving individuals who are willing to end silence, avoidance, and stigma. Potential problems with gatekeepers can be solved when compassionate people are trained in suicide first aid. Caring spiritual leaders who focus on humane and thoughtful treatment of others can be formed and found in the local congregation. Gatekeeping needs love-soaked people to practice the model, and congregations need to practice gatekeeping to save suicidal people.

Churches could have a vital role in solving the public health crisis that suicide represents, and these seven steps can help congregations address the pain and hurt of at-risk individuals. People should ask, "Is my church prepared to save lives?" There are wounded people just outside the door, and while it may not be obvious, there are also wounded people inside the church doors. Suicide exists in our congregations. It is already present in the community where we worship. People are struggling, isolated, and alone. The needs may be hidden, but they are present in every church building. Is there something that congregations can do differently? I believe that these seven steps can move us toward a better solution to care for people. We all have a spiritual hunger that the world cannot satisfy. Jesus came to seek and save the lost. Everyone needs to be a part of a community to have a sense of belonging and connection. Congregations are the ideal place for this fellowship to be experienced. Here, people discover their true value and worth. They can also experience a loving group of people who want the best for them. It is within a caring community of believers that people can learn best that they are loved unconditionally by God. The church is called to be a faith-filled community who cares about God and broken people, and as such, it must realign to support recovery and wellness. I believe congregations are up to the challenge. Engaging these steps allows us to end the silence on suicide by speaking the love of Jesus.

CHAPTER 6
REFLECTION AND CONCLUSION

Personal Thoughts

The exclusion of religion and spirituality from the fight against suicide has caused immense harm. I believe that it is a major contributing factor on why people feel helpless, hopeless, and worthless. I also believe that this exclusion has unnecessarily taken many lives. I have been in meetings where leaders suddenly realize that a vital person is not in the room. Normally, a runner is sent out to find the valued but absent individual and bring them to the table. While there is normally a moment of embarrassment or explanation, the absent individual joins the gathering, and we are all able to finally move forward together. Religion has a place at the table in suicide prevention. In fact, its chair is a place of prominence. Religion and spirituality offer the strongest protection against suicide. Our physical, psychological, and spiritual needs are all distinct, but they are not equal. Religion leads the charge and offers the greatest protection. Clinical epidemiology shows religious and spiritual engagement to be the leading protective factor conferring prevention against suicide (Wu 2015, 1). Moreover, Christians believe that divine grace aids them in helping those with thoughts of suicide.

In like manner, some churches have needlessly hurt many people and families by refusing recognition of medical, psychiatric, psychological, and therapeutic solutions, deeming medicine and science as unnecessary or inappropriate. They turn suicide into a strictly spiritual matter, an approach that completely ignores our physical and mental health needs. Churches with this tactic have developed a subtle Gnosticism by treasuring the spiritual but finding the physical to be an obstacle. This approach has equally tragic consequences as it denies or rejects the physiological needs of depressed individuals and champions only the spiritual health concerns. It has disconnected suicidal people from vital solutions to their own health and wellbeing. It denies the importance of seeing a doctor for physical health, getting medications that can provide mental health, or even talking with a counselor. We find people using ointments, oils, balms, and liquids as medicine for their health in scripture (2 Kings 20:7, Isa. 1:6, Isa. 38:21, Jer. 51:8, 1 Tim. 5:23). In the parable of the Good Samaritan in Luke 10, Jesus describes the Samaritan as someone who lovingly cares for a severely injured man, because he "bandaged up his wounds, pouring oil and wine on them; and he put him on his own beast, and brought him to an inn and took care of him" (Luke 10:34). It is no accident the story is recorded for us here. Luke was a disciple and a doctor.

Taking medicine is not a failure to place your faith and trust in God. It is not a sin. Using medical means for health and wellness is a biblical model for us to follow. God can use medicine to heal and restore our bodies. Prayer is not the only item on the menu. Lund (2014) claims that "Faith is not an anti-depressant. It cannot be swallowed in order to rewire our brains for happiness" (75). Mental illness is a real medical condition just like diabetes. Some people cannot regulate the chemical needs of the brain; others cannot regulate the chemical needs of their pancreas or liver. Methods like medicine and therapy are real solutions that can move people toward greater health and wellness. Followers of Jesus must create a third integrative approach to caring for people, one that forms and supports integrating scripture and the sciences. Churches need to embrace the physical, mental, and spiritual aspects of our humanity to address suicide. If congregations will support an integrative approach, it will move people toward wellbeing.

Christianity is more than mental ascent or believing the proper things about Jesus. The message of Jesus was not just the forgiveness of sins but also the newness of life. To be "saved" means that Jesus "rescued us from the domain of darkness, and transferred us to the Kingdom of his beloved Son," (Col. 1:13). Willard (1991) explains, "We who are saved are to have a different order of life from that of the unsaved. We are to live in a different 'world'" (37). We fail to understand the message of Christianity if we fail to understand the meaning of new life. Willard also explains it this way: "If a convert's habits remain the same, they will realize little of the life in Christ" (114). Paul picks this up as a call for the Christian to become in experience what he or she already is in position: dead to sin and alive to God. He said, "And do not go on presenting the members of your body to sin as instruments of unrighteousness;

but present yourselves to God as those alive from the dead, and your members as instruments of righteousness to God" (Rom. 6:13). Once you are saved in faith, it is time to start your Christian walk and witness. As this may require using new or weak spiritual muscles, the first steps of faith may prove to be wobbly and unsure. Willard illustrates it this way: "Discipline, strictly speaking, is activity carried on to prepare us indirectly for some activity other than itself. We do not practice the piano to practice the piano well, but to play it well" (1991, 120). How we perform our faith and Christian walk does matter. The old person and old ways cannot remain. If mental ascent is the only factor addressed in faith, then there would be no effort or striving after a new righteous life.

The large number of people forsaking the church is also tragic, as we see more people disengaging from religion and congregations across the country. Religious affiliations are down, and negative opinions of the church are up. People do not want to attend churches or participate with congregations. They want nothing to do with God. Part of this is easy to explain. Non-Christians do not want to go to church because the people there do not reflect Jesus. Many Christians are not Christ-like. Some Christians do not resemble Jesus at all, and they sour unchurched people on religion and God. Remember that even those outside of the church know how Christians are supposed to act and behave. It is not a secret. If unchurched people sense a phony Christian in their midst, it gives churches a black eye and speaks poorly of the Christian lifestyle. There is a real danger to nominal Christianity becoming normal Christianity. If Christians are not love-soaked people, then outsiders can easily argue for avoiding them and their acquaintances. Christians who do not demonstrate grace or a lifestyle of love ultimately drive people away from the church and from God. Loving or not loving people is a window into our relationship with Jesus. In a time when people demand authentic community, less than loving people keep unchurched individuals from participating in a congregation. We must open the doors of our heart to Jesus before we can open the doors of the church to hurting people. Willard and Black (2014) help to explain the problem:

The Bible, Christian history, and careful observation all attest to the fact that the Christian movement in general, and specifically during the period of the first century, drastically and intentionally transformed its world. However, today study after study shows that the character and lifestyle of ordinary Christians in North America does not differ significantly from those of non-Christians. Christianity Today reported on a study conducted by the Barna Group that compared Christian to non-Christian lifestyles. The director of the study, David Kinnaman, summarized his findings with this sad analysis: "The respect, patience, self-control and kindness of born-again Christians should astound people, but the lifestyles and relationships of born-again believers are not much different than [those of] others." (Black, 51)

Many Christians show no evidence of God's radical grace and love in their life. Their lifestyles and relationships reflect that of the world, not our loving Lord. If a Christian life shows no contrast to the world, then that life points people to something other than Jesus. The body of Christ must help to usher in the Kingdom of God through a Christian example that is real, authentic, and transforming. Everyone must participate in living the Christian way that sets us apart from the world.

Jesus is not the church. On the other hand, the church represents Jesus. It is the local expression of God's Kingdom. It is formed with renewed and transformed people who follow Jesus. The earthly idea of killing Jesus was that he would not be heard from again; this would stop the movement he created. It was, instead, like blowing on a dandelion. It scattered seeds all over the Earth. Jesus did not come to change the world on his own, but together, with a people around him who could go out and do the work of God with him. Working in tandem with God speaks to the importance and necessity of what people do with their time. Now is the time to rouse the church from its silent slumber on suicide and provide care to hurting people. May we continue, by God's grace, in the path of the first-century church, to share the message and live in a manner worthy of Christ.

This is a heightened time to combat suicide where we live. People are hurting even more due to the challenges of COVID-19. Mark Czeisler says, "The coronavirus disease 2019 (COVID-19) pandemic has been associated with mental health challenges related to the morbidity and mortality caused by the disease and to mitigation activities, including the impact of physical distancing and stay-at-home orders." Mental health concerns have been expressed for much of the year, but studies are just beginning to record the size and scope of the pandemic's impact. A CDC (Centers for Disease Control and Prevention) survey taken during June 24-30, 2020, found that nearly 41% of the 5,412 people reported "at least one adverse mental or behavioral health condition." (2020, 1049). The pandemic and mitigation activities now show elevated adverse mental health conditions. Figure 4 shows that anxiety, depression, substance use, and suicide report higher levels compared to last year.

Figure 4.

Struggles Surge during the 2020 Pandemic

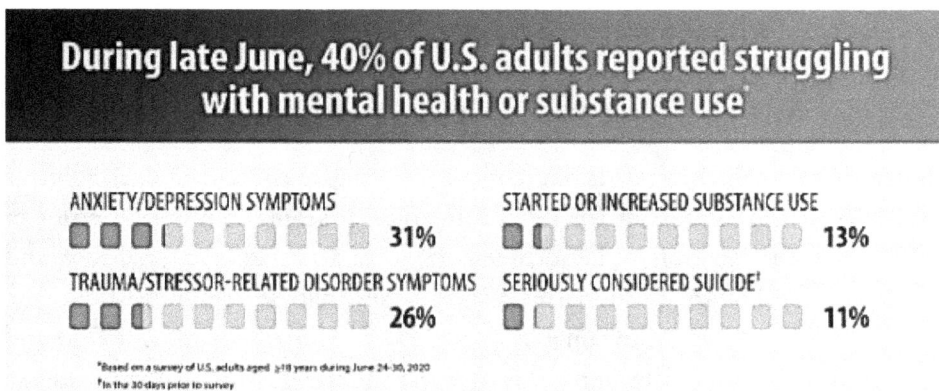

During late June, 40% of U.S. adults reported struggling with mental health or substance use*

ANXIETY/DEPRESSION SYMPTOMS
31%

STARTED OR INCREASED SUBSTANCE USE
13%

TRAUMA/STRESSOR-RELATED DISORDER SYMPTOMS
26%

SERIOUSLY CONSIDERED SUICIDE[†]
11%

*Based on a survey of U.S. adults aged ≥18 years during June 24-30, 2020
[†] In the 30 days prior to survey

(Czeisler 1049).

The highest percentage of people who seriously considered suicide thirty days prior to the survey was significantly higher among respondents aged 18–24 years at 25.5%, self-reported unpaid caregivers for adults at 30.7%, and essential workers at 21.7% (1049). These three categories represent an elevated threat of suicidal ideation and behavior. The CDC report specifically pointed out that now is a critical time to address suicide at local levels. Czeisler notes, "Community-level intervention and prevention efforts, including health communication strategies, designed to reach these groups could help address various mental health conditions associated with the COVID-19 pandemic" (2020, 1050). Now is the time for action. Now is the time to show love for our neighbor. Now is the perfect time for congregations to end their silence and respond to hurting people. Increased social isolation seems to be the new normal. People feel even more helpless and hopeless than before the pandemic began. Now, is the time to seek out those suffering with thoughts of suicide and provide community. The need to rise up and address suicide is greater than we could possibly imagine.

Christianity is strongly against suicide. It carries a proscription on self-destruction due to the core beliefs of Christianity. God communicates through scripture and biblical principles that suicide is not His will for us. God is not a fan of suicide. We are made in a unique fashion that demands preservation. Murder and suicide contradict the priceless worth that God has placed on every human being. Christianity does not encourage suicide because the act communicates that there is no answer for despair. This is the opposite of the love, grace, and compassion we find in the gospel message.

Suggesting that the Bible does not condemn or condone suicide is overly simple and misses God's guidance for all of humanity. It seems to miss the point of scriptural interpretation and ethical lessons and narratives from scripture, and it runs counter to the gospel. The Bible teaches that people are made in the image of God and are of invaluable worth. Destroying life displeases God and runs counter to his holy example. Murder and the self-destructive act of suicide are wrong. This is not a new teaching but an ancient lesson established long before Moses shared the Ten Commandments.

Scripture gives a narrative of hope, healing, and resurrection. While we find many examples of despairing prophets, priests, and ministers of God, they are later reminded to follow after the Lord no matter what their circumstances may be. God does not stop loving us even if he feels distant to us. God loves us in spite of our weaknesses and imperfections. In fact, these times of failure show that we serve a God of second, third, and fourth chances, one who beckons and encourages us to come ever closer to him regardless of our own shortcomings. There is transformational power in the Christian faith. This unconditional love changes us and moves us to become love-soaked people who embody the Kingdom of God.

Conclusion

Religion and spirituality have much to offer in the fight against suicide. Scripture, spiritual practices, and congregations can speak to the needs of people contemplating suicide. When people feel helpless, hopeless, and worthless they can always turn to God. Jesus is with you even if your situation feels unbearable. If people would examine scripture, then they would find a story of love and hope, an amazing story wherein God wants us to build a relationship and stay in fellowship with him. If people would utilize spiritual practices and spiritual formation techniques, they could discover an efficient way to come closer to God. They would also discover a powerful way to buffer themselves from suicide. If people increase religious practices, engage in worship activities, and religious involvement, then they would participate in the strongest protective factors against suicide that science can record. Churches and congregations can also stem the tide of suicide where we live. If congregations would return to the notion of baking good bread, it would provide a model for creating love-soaked people and drawing unchurched individuals. Making time for discipleship and spiritual growth go far to alleviate much of the pain and suffering of suicide. Faith can change the trajectory of our lives.

The Bible teaches that people are of incredible value and worth. Life must not be thrown away or discarded. Our lives matter to friends and family. Our lives also matter to God. This understanding is vital. We are loved, treasured, and valued beyond measure. Realizing the depth of God's care for us can create hope, purpose, and a new life with the Lord. Suffering and hardship are real. Pain and sorrow may not easily go away. Difficult times reveal the truth about people and what they believe. We may not fully realize the power and availability of God until we are suffering, persecuted, or under tribulation. It takes incredible strength to stand firm in the storms of life and cast our reliance on the almighty, but this is what we are all called to do.

The Bible is essentially a love letter from God. It is a written guarantee that we are never alone, forsaken, or forgotten. Anytime we feel lost, hopeless, full of despair, or have doubts, we can go back to the written word for reassurance.

Scripture shows us many examples of people who were depressed but chose life. Moses, Job, Elijah, Jonah, and Jeremiah all felt hopeless during different times in their life. Scripture also records women who thought about killing themselves and instead chose life: Rebekah (Gen. 27:46) and Rachel (Gen. 30:1). The Book of Psalms records many examples of despair, despondency, and pleas for deliverance. Even though David frequently experienced darkness and isolation, he decided to follow God. Simon Peter denies Jesus three times and is terribly distraught by what he has done. Scripture records that Peter runs away and weeps bitterly (Matt. 26:69-75). In this moment of crisis, we can easily imagine Peter as a broken man with nothing to live for. How should he respond to this failure of discipleship? Peter shows us that the best response to failure is repentance, not sorrow unto death like Judas. We see that anyone can start again after a personal failure, no matter the size and scope of the wrong committed, no matter how bad a situation may seem. We can turn to God in our sorrow and our shame, and God will comfort and encourage us as well as guide and empower us. God does not want any to perish by suicide but to rejoin and restore relationship with him. With the grace of God, Christians are called to remain steadfast in the midst of trials (2 Cor. 12:7-10; Phil. 4:11-13; James 1:2-4). The entire story of scripture is redemption and restoration for those who will confess and turn back to a loving, gracious God.

Spiritual practices deliver spiritual strength. They enable individuals to connect with God and grow into love-soaked people. Spiritually, we should not stop growing. While our physical bodies reach a final height or stature, our spiritual body can never grow enough. We are called to continually grow in faith, hope, and love, aided by the grace of God's Holy Spirit. Religious involvement and engagement give hope and purpose to those who are hurting internally. The darkness subsides and we find remnants of the Lord's tender mercy. Living our faith reminds us that we are not alone. Daily spiritual exercise allows us to grow in faith. Religion and spirituality are strong protections against suicide. Robins outlined how "Evidence supports the conclusion that religiousness is associated with lower levels of suicidal ideation, suicide attempts, and even death by suicide" (2009, 387). The unchurched, or those with no faith, are at greater risk of suicide. Those who engage their faith have a brighter hope for tomorrow. They are also supported and connected by a caring community of faith. Beautrais (2005) shares how faith combats suicide:

> Religious affiliation and religious activity exert a protective effect in a number of ways, including proscribing against suicide and promoting social links, with these links and prohibitions also decreasing the risk of psychiatric disorders (including depression, substance abuse, offending and antisocial behaviours) with which suicide is associated. (37-38)

Congregations and churches, which Christians believe are aided by the Holy Spirit, are the vehicle for change in suicide prevention. Their servant spirit and gracious activity are needed to transform a hurting world. When congregations offer assistance, community, and fellowship, they foster feelings of comfort and warmth to suicidal people. Their love and compassion are needed in every neighborhood and community. Congregations can offer something greater than that which the world can offer. They offer hurting people the fruit of the spirit – of God's Holy Spirit: love, joy, peace, patience, kindness, goodness, faithfulness, gentleness, and self-control (Gal. 5:22-23). When congregations provide love and care, they communicate that at-risk people matter, even if they cannot see or feel it at that moment in time. Congregations offer a place to belong, connect, and grow. Churches must be a warm and engaging place where all are welcome to participate in the way of Jesus. These practices mean that the stranger in our midst is not a consumer of entertainment but a person who deeply needs the love of God. I believe that there is a reason why mental health consumers and people at risk of suicide come to clergy and church leaders before clinicians and counselors. Congregations are filled with love-soaked people who embody the Kingdom of God. Churches can provide the necessary advantage our world needs in suicide prevention. Churches must be silent no more; that is a Christian response to suicide.

Suicide is more than a public health threat; it is a cry for help. The sad, the lonely, and the suffering want something more than what they can find in this world. Jesus can speak to their need. Loving and compassionate people are now required to stand in the gap and support those at risk of suicide. The Christian faith has unique tools of scripture, spiritual practices, and congregational care to combat suicide, all of which are aided by God's grace. The church can reflect Jesus by returning to the original blueprint of a carpenter from Nazareth. It is here where we learn how to make love-soaked people who will embody the Kingdom of God. I believe that the church is up to the task of providing hope, love, and life in our society. If we will end our silence on suicide, then we can connect hurting people with the Savior and Redeemer of the world.

REFERENCES

American Association of Suicidology. February 12, 2020. Accessed June 1, 2020. https://suicidology.org/facts-and-statistics/.

American Psychiatric Association Foundation. *Mental Health: A Guide for Faith Leaders.* Arlington, VA: American Psychiatric Association Foundation, 2016.

Augsburger, David. *Dissident Discipleship: A Spirituality of Self-Surrender, Love of God, and Love of Neighbor.* Grand Rapids, MI: Brazos Press, 2006.

Baltimore Catechism #3 "Lesson 33 - From the Fourth to the Seventh Commandment." Accessed December 17, 2020. http://www.baltimore-catechism.com/ lesson33.htm.

Barry, William. *Finding God in All Things.* Notre Dame, IN: Ave Maria Press, 1991.

Bates, Josiah. "Megachurch Pastor and Mental Health Advocate Jarrid Wilson Dies by Suicide." *Time.* September 11, 2019. https://time.com/5674636/megachurch-pastor-jarrid-wilson-dies-suicide/.

Beautrais A. L., S. C. Collings, and P. Ehrhardt. *Suicide Prevention: A Review of Evidence of Risk and Protective Factors, and Points of Effective Intervention.* Wellington, New Zealand: Ministry of Health, 2005.

Black, Gary, Jr. *The Theology of Dallas Willard.* Eugene, OR: Pickwick Publications, 2013.

Bonezzi C., L. Demartini, and M. Buonocore. "Chronic Pain: Not Only a Matter of Time." *Minerva Anestesiol* 78, no. 6 (June 2012): 704-711.

Bonhoeffer, Dietrich. *Life Together*. Translated by John W. Doberstein. San Francisco, CA: Harper, 1993.

The Book of Common Prayer and Administration of the Sacraments and Other Rites and Ceremonies of the Church: Together with the Psalter or Psalms of David According to the Use of the Episcopal Church. New York, NY: Seabury Press, 1979.

Brand, Chad, Charles Draper, and Archie England, eds. *Holman Illustrated Bible Dictionary*. Nashville, TN: Holman Bible Publishers, 2003.

Burnette, Crystal, Rajeev Ramchand, and Lynsay Ayer. "Gatekeeper Training for Suicide Prevention: A Theoretical Model and Review of the Empirical Literature." *Rand Health Quarterly* 5, no. 1 (July 2015): 1-20.

Calhoun, Adele Ahlberg. *Spiritual Disciplines Handbook: Practices that Transform Us*. Downers Grove, IL: IVP Books, 2015.

Catechism of the Catholic Church. 2nd ed. Washington, D.C.: United States Catholic Conference, 2019.

Centers for Disease Control and Prevention. Web-Based Injury Statistics Query and Reporting System (WISQARS). Atlanta, GA: National Center for Injury Prevention and Control. Accessed June 1, 2020. http://www.cdc.gov/injury/ wisqars/index.html.

Clemons, James T. *What Does the Bible Say about Suicide?* Minneapolis, MN: Augsburg Fortress, 1990.

Closson, David. "What Does It Mean to Be Made in God's Image?" The Ethics & Religious Liberty Commission of the Southern Baptist Convention. May 4, 2016. Accessed June 1, 2020. https://erlc.com/ resource-library/articles/what-does-it-mean-to-be-made-in-gods-image.

Cooley, Dennis R. "Was Jesus an Assisted Suicide?" *Ethics, Medicine, and Public Health* 14, Article 100514 (July-September 2020): 1-10.

Cooperman, Alan. "*When Americans Say They Believe in God, What Do They Mean?*" Washington, D.C.: Pew Research Center, 2018.

Czeisler, M. É., R. I. Lane, and E. Petrosky et al. "Mental Health, Substance Use, and Suicidal Ideation during the COVID-19 Pandemic – United States, June 24-30, 2020." *MMWR Morbidity and Mortality Weekly Report* 69, no. 32 (August 2020): 1049–1057.

De La Vega Sanchez, Diego, Julio Guija, Pedro Perez-Moreno, Samuel A. Kelley, Maria Santos, Maria Oquendo, Philippe Courtet, Jose Giner, and Lucas Giner. "Association of Religious Activity with Male Suicide Deaths." *Suicide and Life-Threatening Behavior* 50, no. 2 (April 2020): 449-460.

Demy, Timothy J. and Gary P. Stewart, eds. *Suicide: A Christian Response*. Grand Rapids, MI: Kregel Publications, 1998.

Drapeau, Christopher W., and John L. McIntosh. "U.S.A. Suicide: 2018 Official Final Data." American Association of Suicidology. February 12, 2020. Accessed June 1, 2020. https://suicidology.org/facts-and-statistics/.

Evangelical Friends Church – Mid America Yearly Meeting. *Faith and Practice: The Book of Discipline*. September 2, 2019. Accessed September 11, 2020. https://efcmaym.org/about/faith-and-practice/

Fetzer Institute. *Multidimensional Measurement of Religiousness / Spirituality for Use in Health Research: A Report of the Fetzer Institute / National Institute on Aging Working Group*. Kalamazoo, MI: Fetzer Institute, 2003.

Gardner, Steve. "Cardinals reliever Jordan Hicks throws MLB's fastest pitch at 105 mph." USA Today. May 20, 2018. https://www.usatoday.com/story/sports/mlb/ cardinals/2018/05/ 20/cardinals-jordan-hicks-ties-mlb-record-throwing-105-mph-twice/627391002/.

Guyon, Jeanne. *Experiencing the Depths of Jesus Christ*. Auburn, ME: The Seedsowers, 1975.

Harris, Rachel S. "Samson's Suicide: Death and the Hebrew Literary Canon." *Israel Studies* 17, no. 3 (Fall 2012): 67-91.

Hauerwas, Stanley. "The Morality of Suicide: Issues and Options," by J. P. Moreland. In *Suicide: A Christian Response,* edited by Timothy J. Demy and Gary P. Stewart, 190. Grand Rapids, MI: Kregel Publications, 1998.

Henderson, D. Michael. *John Wesley's Class Meeting: A Model for Making Disciples*. Wilmore, KY: Rafiki Books, 2016.

Howsepian, A. A. "Some Reservations about Suicide." In *Suicide: A Christian Response*, edited by Timothy J. Demy and Gary P. Stewart, 300. Grand Rapids, MI: Kregel Publications, 1998.

Hsu, Albert. In "The Truth about Suicide." Lee, Morgan. *Christianity Today.* October 20, 2017. https://www.christianitytoday.com/ct/2017/november/suicide-americans-taking-their-own-lives-church-al-hsu.html.

Hunter, James David. *To Change The World: The Irony, Tragedy, and Possibility of Christianity in the Late Modern World*. New York, NY: Oxford University Press, 2010.

Idler, Ellen and Linda George. "What Sociology Can Help Us Understand About Religion and Mental Health." In *Handbook of*

Religion and Mental Health, edited by Harold G. Koenig, 53. San Diego, CA: Academic Press, 1998.

Jobes, David A. *Managing Suicidal Risk: A Collaborative Approach*. New York, NY: The Guilford Press, 2006.

Johnson, Eric L. *God and Soul Care: The Therapeutic Resources of the Christian Faith*. Downers Grove, IL: IVP Academic, 2017.

Johnson, Jan. *When the Soul Listens: Finding Rest and Direction in Contemplative Prayer*. Colorado Springs, CO: NavPress, 2017.

Joiner, T. E., Jr., K. A. Van Orden, T. K. Witte, and M. D. Rudd. *The Interpersonal Theory of Suicide: Guidance for Working with Suicidal Clients*. Washington, D.C.: American Psychological Association, 2009.

Kaplan, Kalman J., and Paul Cantz. *Biblical Psychotherapy: Reclaiming Scriptural Narratives for Positive Psychology and Suicide Prevention*. Lanham, MD: Lexington Books, 2017.

Kaplan, Kalman J., and Matthew B. Schwartz. *A Psychology of Hope: A Biblical Response to Tragedy and Suicide*. Grand Rapids, MI: Eerdmans Publishing Co., 2008.

Keefe, Rachael A. *The Lifesaving Church: Faith Communities and Suicide Prevention*. Saint Louis, MO: Chalice Press, 2018.

Keener, Craig S. *The IVP Bible Background Commentary: New Testament*. Downers Grove, IL: InterVarsity Press, 1993.

Keller, Jared. "The U.S. Suicide Rate Is at Its Highest in a Half-Century." *Pacific Standard*. December 4, 2018. https://psmag.com/news/the-suicide-rate-is-at-its-highest-in-a-half-century.

Kheriaty, Aaron. "Dying of Despair." *First Things* 275 (August/ September, 2017): 21-25.

Koenig, Harold G., ed. *Handbook of Religion and Mental Health.* San Diego, CA: Academic Press, 1998.

_____. "Religion, Spirituality, and Health: The Research and Clinical Implications." *ISRN Psychiatry* 2012, Article ID 278730 (December, 2012): 1-33.

LivingWorks Education. *Applied Suicide Intervention Skills Training Participant Workbook.* Calgary, Canada: LivingWorks, 2014.

Lund, Sarah Griffith. *Blessed Are the Crazy: Breaking the Silence about Mental Illness, Family, and Church.* Saint Louis, MO: Chalice Press, 2014.

Maas, Robin, and Gabriel O'Donnell, eds. *Spiritual Traditions for the Contemporary Church.* Nashville, TN: Abingdon Press, 1990.

Mason, Karen. *Preventing Suicide: A Handbook for Pastors, Chaplains and Pastoral Counselors.* Downers Grove, IL: IVP Books, 2014.

Masten, Ann S. "Ordinary Magic: Resilience Processes in Development," *American Psychologist* 56, no. 3 (2001): 227-238.

Mazrui, Ali. "Sacred Suicide." *Transition.* No. 21, (1965): 10-15. DOI: 10.2307/2934092

McKnight, Scot. *A Community Called Atonement.* Nashville, TN: Abingdon Press, 2007.

Merrill, Eugene H. "Suicide and the Concept of Death in the Old Testament." In *Suicide: A Christian Response*, edited by Timothy J. Demy and Gary P. Steart, 323-24. Grand Rapids, MI: Kregel Publications, 1998.

Moll, Rob. *What Your Body Knows About God*. Downers Grove, IL: IVP Books, 2014.

Moreland, J. P. *Finding Quiet*. Grand Rapids, MI: Zondervan, 2019.

National Action Alliance for Suicide Prevention. *Best Practices in Care Transitions for Individuals with Suicide Risk: Inpatient Care to Outpatient Care*. Washington, D.C.: Education Development Center, Inc., 2019.

National Institute for Mental Health. "Suicide." Accessed August 5, 2019. https://www.nimh.nih.gov/health/statistics/suicide.shtml.

Nouwen, Henri. *The Way of the Heart: Connecting with God through Prayer, Wisdom, and Silence*. New York: Ballantine Books, 1981.

O'Mathuna, Donal, "But The Bible Doesn't Say They Were Wrong To Commit Suicide, Does It?" In *Suicide: A Christian Response*, edited by Timothy J. Demy and Gary P. Steart, 348-353. Grand Rapids, MI: Kregel Publications, 1998.

Park, Han Nah, Kaye Cook, Sara E. LePine, and Catherine Steininger. "Do Nonreligious Individuals Have the Same Mental Health and Well-being Benefits as Religious Individuals?" *Journal of Psychology and Christianity* 38, no. 2 (2019): 81-99.

Pope, Charles. "Salutary Repentance." *Our Sunday Visitor News*. December 17, 2018. https://www.osvnews.com/2018/12/17/salutary-repentance/.

Post, Stephen. "Ethics, Religion, and Mental Health." In *Handbook of Religion and Mental Health*, edited by Harold G. Koenig. San Diego, CA: Academic Press, 1998.

Plante, Thomas G. "Integrating Spirituality and Psychotherapy: Ethical Issues and Principles to Consider." *Journal of Clinical Psychology* 63, no. 9 (2007), 891-902.

Post, Stephen. "Ethics, Religion, and Mental Health." In *Handbook of Religion and Mental Health,* edited by Harold G. Koenig. San Diego, CA: Academic Press, 1998.

U.S. Department of Health and Human Services (HHS) Office of the Surgeon General and National Action Alliance for Suicide Prevention. *2012 National Strategy for Suicide Prevention: Goals and Objectives for Action*. Washington, D.C.: HHS, September 2012.

Ramsay, Richard F., Bryan L. Tanney, William A. Lang, and Tarie Kinzel. *Suicide Intervention Handbook*. 10th, ed. Calgary, CA: LivingWorks, 2004.

Reivich, Karen J., Martin Seligman, and Sharon McBride. "Master Resilience Training in the US Army." *American Psychologist* 66, no. 1 (2011): 25-34.

Robins, Alee, and Amy Fiske. "Explaining the Relation between Religiousness and Reduced Suicidal Behavior: Social Support Rather Than Specific Beliefs." *Suicide and Life-Threatening Behavior* 39, no. 4 (August 2009): 386-395.

Ryken, Leland. "But The Bible Doesn't Say They Were Wrong To Commit Suicide, Does It?" by Donal O'Mathuna. In *Suicide: A Christian Response*, edited by Timothy J. Demy and Gary P. Steart, 362. Grand Rapids, MI: Kregel Publications, 1998.

Schaeffer, Francis A. *The Mark of the Christian*. Downers Grove, IL: IVP Books, 2006.

Schlein, Lisa. "More People Die from Suicide than from Wars, Natural Disasters Combined." *VOA News*. September 4, 2014. https://www.voanews.com/science-health/more-people-die-suicide-wars-natural-disasters-combined.

Sheldrake, Philip. *A Brief History of Spirituality*. Oxford, UK: Blackwell Publishing, 2007.

Simpson, Amy. *Troubled Minds: Mental Illness and the Church's Mission*. Downers Grove, IL: IVP Books, 2013.

Stack, Steven. "Religious Activities and Suicide Prevention: A Gender Specific Analysis." *Religions* 9, no. 4 (2018): 1-12.

Stanford, Matthew. *Grace for the Afflicted: A Clinical and Biblical Perspective on Mental Illness*. Downers Grove, IL: IVP Books, 2008.

Stone, Deb M., et al. *Preventing Suicide: A Technical Package of Policies, Programs, and Practices*. Atlanta, GA: National Center for Injury Prevention and Control, Centers for Disease Control and Prevention. 2017.

Strong, James. *Strong's Exhaustive Concordance of the Bible*. Nashville, TN: Thomas Nelson Publishers, 1996.

Suicide Prevention Resource Center. *Choosing a Suicide Prevention Gatekeeper Training Program – A Comparison Table*. Waltham, MA: Education Development Center, Inc., 2018.

Suicide Prevention Resource Center. *Selecting and Implementing a Gatekeeper Training*. Waltham, MA: Education Development Center, Inc., 2020.

Svob, Connie, Priya Wickramaratne, Linda Reich, et al. "Association of Parent and Offspring Religiosity with Offspring Suicide Ideation and Attempts." *JAMA Psychiatry* 75, no. 10 (2018): 1062-1070.

Waitz-Kudla, Sydney N., Samantha E. Daruwala, Claire Houtsma, and Michael D. Anestis. "Help-seeking Behavior in Socially Conservative and Christian Suicide Decedents." *Suicide and Life-Threatening Behavior* 49, no. 6 (December 2019): 1513-1522.

Walton, John H., Victor H. Matthews, and Mark W. Chavalas. *The IVP Bible Background Commentary: Old Testament.* Downers Grove, IL: InterVarsity Press, 2000.

Willard, Dallas. "Essentia Dei and The Protoevangelical." In *The Theology of Dallas* Willard by Gary Black, Jr. Eugene, OR: Pickwick Publications, 2013.

Willard, Dallas. *Hearing God.* Downers Grove, IL: InterVarsity Press, 1999.

_____. *Spirit of the Disciplines: Understanding How God Changes Lives.* SanFrancisco, CA: HarperSanFrancisco, 1991.

_____. *The Great Omission: Reclaiming Jesus's Essential Teachings on Discipleship.* San Francisco, CA: HarperSanFrancisco, 2006.

Willard, Dallas, and Gary Black, Jr. *The Divine Conspiracy Continued: Fulfilling God's Kingdom on Earth.* New York, NY: HarperCollins Publishers, 2014.

Wilson, William P. "Religion and Psychoses." In *Handbook of Religion and Mental Health,* edited by Harold G. Koenig. San Diego, CA: Academic Press, 1998.

World Health Organization. *Preventing Suicide: A Global Imperative.* Geneva, Switzerland: WHO Press, 2014. Mental Health and Substance Use. August 17, 2014. https://www.who.int/publications/i/item/preventing-suicide-a-global-imperative.

_____."Suicide Prevention." Accessed August 5, 2019. https://www.who.int/ mental_health/prevention/suicide/suicideprevent/en/.

Wu, Andrew, Jing-Yu Wang, and Cun-Xian Jia. "Religion and Completed Suicide: A Meta-Analysis." *PLOS ONE.* 10, no. 6 (2015): 1-14.

Wu, Gang, et al. "Understanding Resiliency." *Frontiers in Behavioral Neuroscience* 10 (February 2013): 1-15.

Yangarber-Hicks, Natalia, et al. "Invitation to the Table Conversation: A Few Diverse Perspectives on Integration." *Journal of Psychology and Christianity* 25, no. 4, (Winter 2006): 338-353.

Zahnd, Brian. *Water to Wine: Some of My Story*. Spello Press, 2016.

APPENDIX
DEFINITIONS AND USE OF TERMS

Agape

A Greek word describing a divine form of love. Such a love described in the scriptures is generally assumed to convey moral goodwill and esteem for oneself and others that proceeds from high principle or duty, rather than attraction or charm. Such a love is underserving, despite disappointment and rejection and, therefore, is unconditional in both nature and affect (Black 235).

American Association of Suicidology

AAS is a nonprofit organization that promotes research, public awareness programs, public education, and training for professionals and volunteers. It serves as a national clearinghouse for information on suicide, publishing and disseminating statistics, and suicide prevention resources.

Anthropology

The multitude of methods areas of study related to both the individual human being and humanity at large (Black 2013, 235).

Behavioral health

A state of mental/emotional being and/or choices and actions that affect wellness. Behavioral health problems include substance abuse or misuse, alcohol and drug addiction, serious psychological distress, suicide, and mental and substance use disorders. The term is also used to describe the service systems encompassing the promotion of emotional health; the prevention of mental and substance use disorders, substance use, and related problems; treatments and services for mental and substance use disorders; and recovery support (HHS 138).

Bereaved by suicide

Family members, friends, and others affected by the suicide of a loved one, also referred to as survivors of suicide (HHS 138).

Best practices

Activities or programs that are in keeping with the best available evidence regarding what is effective (HHS 138).

Caring contacts

Cards, notes, letters, and messages sent to people after being discharged from an inpatient hospitalization. Caring contacts research started with Dr. Jerry Motto, a psychiatrist at the University of California, San Francisco. During 1969 to 1974, his caring contact postcard model cut suicide rates in half. Today, the CDC recommends caring contacts and healthcare professionals all across the country send out colorful postcards with positive messages to those at risk of suicide.

Church

The Christian religious community as a whole or a body of local Christian believers. Church can also refer to a congregation.

Chronic pain

Chronic pain, as opposed to the short-lived acute pain, may extend from months to many years, continuing long beyond the typical time required for the injury or illness to be repaired. Pain that persists beyond a three-month period is the most agreed upon distinction. The two most commonly used markers are three months and six months since the initiation of pain, though some theorists and researchers have placed the transition from acute to chronic pain at twelve months (Bonezzi 2012, 705).

Clergy

Formal and official leaders within established religions. They are the religious professionals who conduct rituals, rites, sacraments, services, and counseling for congregants or parishioners. Clergy are ordained by an ecclesiastic authority, a religious body, or group of superiors. They are ordained, recorded, and or licensed to perform pastoral and sacerdotal functions within a religious community. Normally distinct from laity or lay leaders.

Connectedness

The degree to which an individual or group of individuals are socially close, interrelated, or share resources with others (Stone 27). As an example, connections can be formed among individuals, neighbors, coworkers, families, and faith communities.

Consumer

A preferred way of referring to a person who is getting mental healthcare, because it is a nonjudgmental word with less stigma (Lund 105).

Contagion

A phenomenon wherein susceptible persons are influenced toward suicidal behavior through knowledge of another person's suicidal acts (HHS 139).

Epidemiology

The study of statistics and trends in health and disease across communities (HHS 139).

Evidence-based programs

Programs that have undergone scientific evaluation and have proven to be effective (HHS 139).

Gatekeeper

Individuals in a community who have face-to-face contact with large numbers of community members as part of their usual routine. They may be trained to identify persons at risk of suicide and refer them to treatment or supporting services as appropriate. Examples include clergy, first responders, pharmacists, caregivers, and those employed in institutional settings, such as schools, prisons, and the military (HHS 139).

Gatekeeping

Refers to performing the trained responsibilities of a gatekeeper. Military and civilian literature defines the notion of a gatekeeper similarly, although the persons designated as potential gatekeepers across populations vary (Burnette 2). Gatekeeping programs often occur in educational, healthcare, medical, and military settings.

Gnostic

One who believes in Gnosticism, Gnostic thought, or Gnostic concepts. Gnostics believe that the human spirit is more important than the human body.

Gnosticism

An ancient teaching that the spirit is more important than the body. Gnostics believed that the human spirit was naturally good and that matter – physical bodies included – was naturally evil. Gnosticism's radical distinction between spirit and body spilled into early Christian teaching about Jesus and was declared a heresy. Gnostics rejected the idea of Jesus becoming incarnate, dying on the cross, and rising bodily or his resurrection. The Gnostics believed that when Jesus came to Earth, he didn't possess a body; instead, he only seemed to have a physical body.

Hippocampus

A complex brain structure deep in the temporal lobe. This region of the brain is deeply associated with memory, learning, and regulating emotional responses. It is one of the most sensitive parts of the brain. It is also one of the most plastic regions of the brain (Wu 2013, 4).

Homoousion

Greek word that means of one being or of one essence. The Council of Nicaea used this term to describe the divinity of Christ. It is reflected in the Nicene Creed to show that Christians believe Jesus is "one being with the Father."

Hopelessness

The expectation that a negative situation will not get better no matter what one does to change the situation. Hopelessness is intimately linked to future thinking and emphasizes how one perceives self, others, and the future (Jobes 14).

Hypostatic union

The combination of divine and human natures that only exists in Jesus Christ.

Intervention

A strategy or approach that is intended to prevent an outcome or to alter the course of an existing condition. Examples include providing lithium for bipolar disorders, educating providers about suicide prevention, or reducing access to lethal means among individuals with suicide risk (HHS 140).

Koinonia

A Greek word describing community, fellowship, association, partnership, and joint participation (Strong, 50). Koinonia is used twenty different times in the Bible and can be translated many different ways in English. Koinonia can be used for a particular aspect of Christianity, or the dynamic whole of Christian living. It depicts an interactive relationship between God and believers who are sharing new life through Christ. Koinonia is active participation in Christian community.

Martyr

The word was derived from the Greek *martus* or "witness" and was originally applied to the first apostles as witnesses of Jesus (Sheldrake 24). Slowly, it came to be associated with those Christians who suffered hardship for their faith. Eventually, it was limited to those who suffered death (Sheldrake 24).

Means

The instrument or object used to carry out a self-destructive act (HHS 140). Lethal means often describes the device or item used in a suicide or suicide attempt, e.g., chemicals, firearms, medications, illicit drugs.

Means restriction

Techniques, policies, and procedures designed to reduce access or availability to means and methods of deliberate self-harm (HHS 140).

Mental health

The capacity of individuals to interact with one another and the environment in ways that promote subjective well-being, optimal development, and use of mental abilities (cognitive, affective, and relational) (HHS 140).

Mental illness

A disorder of the brain resulting in the disruption of a person's thoughts, feelings, moods, and the ability to relate to others that is severe enough to require psychological or psychiatric intervention (Stanford 43-44). Mental illness is a debilitating experience in which the person is simply unable to function normally over an extended period of time (Stanford 44).

National Center for Injury Prevention and Control or NCIPC

NCIPC, located at the U.S. Centers for Disease Control and Prevention, is a valuable source of information, resources, and statistics about suicide, suicide risk, and suicide prevention. Its website includes links to a number of statistical databases, including WISQARS (Web-based Injury Statistics Query and Reporting System), YRBSS (Youth Risk Behavior Surveillance System), the National Violent Death Reporting System, and the National Vital Statistics System.

National Registry of Evidence-Based Programs and Practices

NREPP is a searchable online registry of roughly 230 interventions and programs supporting mental health promotion, substance abuse prevention, and suicide prevention. The registry connects members of the public to intervention developers so that they can learn how to implement these approaches in their communities.

National Suicide Prevention Lifeline

The Lifeline provides immediate assistance 24 hours a day, 7 days a week to individuals in suicidal crisis by connecting them to the nearest available suicide prevention and mental health service provider through a toll-free telephone number: 1-800-273-TALK (8255). The Lifeline also provides informational materials, such as brochures, wallet cards, posters, and booklets featuring the Lifeline number.

Orthodoxy

Right or accurate belief and or doctrine (Black 2013, 240).

Post-traumatic stress disorder (PTSD)

An anxiety disorder that develops as a result of witnessing or experiencing a traumatic occurrence, especially life-threatening events. PTSD can interfere with a person's ability to hold a job or develop relationships (Koenig 1998, 357).

Postvention

Response to and care for individuals affected in the aftermath of a suicide attempt or suicide death. (HHS 141)

Prayer

Conversation with God. This communication can be spoken or silent. There are many forms and types of prayer, like supplication and intercession. Contemplative prayer focuses on people stopping to listen for what God has to say. Prayer allows people to strengthen their faith and relationship with God. Prayer is considered a spiritual discipline. Clinical studies and research show prayer is a strong coping response that enhances hope and works to prevent suicide (Koenig 1998, 25-27, 123, 132).

Prevention

A strategy or approach that reduces the likelihood of risk of onset or delays the onset of adverse health problems, or reduces the harm resulting from conditions or behaviors (HHS 141).

Protective factors

Characteristics, conditions, or influences that decrease the likelihood of suicide. Protective factors can counter a specific risk factor or buffer against a number of risks associated with suicide (Stone 9).

Psychache

Term coined by Edwin Shneidman to describe intense, unbearable psychological pain that results from significant unmet psychological needs. Psychache is pain, not an illness. When left unresolved, psychache leads to suicide, suicidal thoughts, or suicidal behavior (Keefe 9).

Psychiatry

The medical science that deals with the origin, diagnosis, prevention, and treatment of mental disorders (HHS 141).

Psychology

The science concerned with the individual behavior of humans, including mental and physiological processes related to behavior (HHS 141).

Psychological pain

A profound and seemingly unbearable suffering that exists in the mind's eye of the suicidal person. Also referred to as Shneidman's concept of psychache (Jobes 11).

Religion

The beliefs, practices, and rituals related to the transcendent, where the transcendent is understood as God (Koenig 2012, 2). Religion offers us meaning and provides a narrative of comfort and hope

(Lund, 98). Most religions have rules and regulations, also known as doctrines, about how to live life and how to treat others within a social group (Koenig 2012, 7). Most religions emphasize love of others, compassion, and altruistic acts as well as encourage meeting together during religious social events. Many of the journals, studies, and papers used craft their own definition or understanding of religion. I write and describe religion from a Christian context.

Resilience

A set of processes that enable good outcomes in spite of serious threats (Masten 227). The ability to persist in the face of challenges and to bounce back from adversity (Reivich 25). Common descriptions of resilience are optimism, problem solving, faith, sense of meaning, self-efficacy, flexibility, impulse control, empathy, close relationships, and spirituality.

Risk factors

Characteristics, conditions, or influences that increase the likelihood of suicide.

Safety plan

Written list of warning signs, coping responses, and support sources that an individual may use to avert or manage a suicide crisis (HHS 142).

Sanctification

The Christian understanding of growing in holiness and conformity to the will of God. Commonly seen as both an event and a process. A Christian is sanctified as an event upon acceptance and belief in Jesus, thereby receiving the Holy Spirit. A Christian experiences sanctification as a process where the individual's will is increasingly surrendered to the will of God (EFC 27).

Screening

Administration of an assessment tool to identify persons in need of more in-depth evaluation or treatment (HHS 142).

Screening tools

Instruments and techniques (e.g., questionnaires, check lists, self-assessment forms) used to evaluate individuals for increased risk of certain health problems (HHS 142).

Self-directed violence

Behavior directed at oneself that deliberately results in injury or the potential for injury. Self-directed violence may be suicidal or non-suicidal in nature (Stone 7).

Social isolation

A state in which an individual lacks a sense of social belonging, engagement with others, and fulfilling relationships.

Spiritual disciplines

Means that allow us to come into contact with God and relate to God. The intentional practices, relationships, and experiences that give people space in their lives to keep company with Jesus (Calhoun 19). Additional terms for these practices include Christian practices, spiritual practices, spiritual exercises, religious practices, rituals, or the disciplines.

Spiritual formation

A whole life process dealing with change in every essential part of the person (Willard 2006, 55). The process of shaping our spirit and giving it a definite character. The formation of our spirit in conformity with the Spirit of Christ (Willard 2006, 53).

Spirituality

In Christian terms, spirituality refers to the way our fundamental values, lifestyles, and spiritual practices reflect particular understandings of God, human identity, and the material world as the context for human transformation (Sheldrake 2). Christianity is the original source of the word, although it has now passed into other faith traditions, not least of which are Eastern religions such as Buddhism and Hinduism (Sheldrake 2).

Spirituality is distinguished by its connection to that which is sacred, divine, or viewed as transcendent. Spirituality is intimately connected to the supernatural, the mystical, and to organized religion, although it may begin without structure or understanding before turning toward organized religion. Spirituality can be both a search for the transcendent and the discovery of the transcendent (Koenig 2012, 3).

Stigma

An undesirable attribute that makes a person different or tainted or inferior (Mason 141). Negative stereotypes and discriminatory behavior against someone who has or is thought to have a mental illness (Burnette 8). Stigma can also be a mark of shame, infamy, or social disapproval. Stigma can result in avoidance, ostracism, and even ridicule.

Substance Abuse and Mental Health Services Administration or SAMHSA

SAMHSA funds and supports the National Suicide Prevention Lifeline, the Suicide Prevention Resource Center, and manages the Garrett Lee Smith Suicide Prevention Program, which funds state, territorial, and tribal programs to prevent suicide among youth. It developed the National Registry of Evidence-based Programs and Practices (NREPP), which reviews evidence of effectiveness for prevention programs on topics related to behavioral health, including suicide.

Suicidal behavior

Any self-destructive act that would include attempt behaviors or suicidal gestures. Can also include any specific behavior preparations for an attempt (e.g., stashing medications) would be considered suicidal behavior (Jobes 102). Suicidal behavior can also describe attempts and suicide deaths.

Suicide

Intentionally ending your own life. A self-inflicted death. Killing yourself. The deliberate ending of one's own life. Self-destruction or self-annihilation. Self-murder.

Suicide attempt

A nonfatal, self-inflicted injury that shows evidence of one's intent to die (Mason 112). A suicide attempt may or may not result in injury. What makes the suicide attempt act is the intent to die, not the physical injury; the injury itself or the medical lethality of the act does not determine whether an act was a suicide attempt.

Suicidal ideation

Thoughts of engaging in suicide-related behavior. (HHS 143).

Suicide intervention

A way of preventing suicide, commonly known as suicide first aid (LivingWorks 5). Increasing the safety of a person or persons with thoughts of suicide. Directly engaging in conversation to discover a person's reasons to die while encouraging life, hope, and safety for now.

Web-Based Injury Statistics Query and Reporting System or WISQARS

An interactive database system that provides customized reports of data from a variety of sources on fatal and nonfatal injuries, violent deaths, and cost of injury. The system features a large amount of data on suicide (HHS 135).

Zero Suicide

The Zero Suicide framework is a system-wide, organizational commitment to safer suicide care in health and behavioral health care systems. The framework is based on the realization that suicidal individuals often fall through the cracks in a sometimes fragmented and distracted health care system. A systematic approach to quality improvement in these settings is both available and necessary (NAASP 19).

Endnotes

[1] Since some versions of scripture do not totally align in translation, terms, names, or numbers, I will use the New American Standard Bible or NASB translation for the entire paper.

[2] There is no unanimity among Christians with regard to the so-called constituent parts of being human. Do people consist of a body and soul? Do they consist of a body, soul, and spirit? Do they consist of a heart, soul, mind, and strength? Are they a complex unity, consisting of a variety of parts? Scripture does not intend to speak definitively about scientific or behavioral scientific matters. As such, the language scripture used to describe people has more theological significance than scientific significance. Interpreters of scripture ought to beware of ontologizing biblical categories used for talking about people at the expense of excluding insights from scientific and behavioral scientific investigations.

[3] Again, there is no unanimity among Christians with regard to the "immaterial" parts of people. For example, is there a mind/body (immaterial/material) dualism, as Descartes suggested? Are the immaterial aspects of mind and spirit reducible to naturalistic materialism, or are they not reducible, as non-reductive physicalism argues? Such debates are not at issue in my discussion of suicide. Suffice it to say that the language of scripture about the various parts of people is sufficient for talking about matters related to suicide, and that use of biblical language does not preclude the integration of insights from science, medicine, and other behavioral sciences.

[4] Some prefer to talk primarily about Jesus as the word of God, as found in John 1:1, and only secondarily are the words of scripture referred to as the word of God (Phil. 2:14-16a, Heb. 4:12). Even the latter verses may be more appropriately considered references to Jesus rather than to scripture. However, such debates are not relevant to the topic of this writing. As such, I talk about scripture as the word of God, or Word of God, which is a traditional Christian way of referring to the Bible.

[5] Obviously, there are multiple views among Christians as well as non-Christians regarding the legal and/or moral justifications for taking a life, that is, killing someone. Without going into those views, suffice it to say that the majority view is that people should not to die by suicide.

[6] Historical and critical scholarship question the reliability of the Noahic stories, along with all of Genesis 1-11. Even if one questions their reliability, Noah is theologically instructive about canonical teachings in Scripture regarding moral decision-making, for example, as related to matters of suicide.

[7] Some interpreters refer to verses like this one in advocating *lex talionis* (Lat., "law of retaliation"), epitomized by the language of an "eye for an eye" (Exod. 21:24). Jesus challenged this logic, advocating neither retaliating nor fleeing, but challenging injustice by non-violent means (Matt. 5:38-42). However, Christians disagree about whether he advocated pacifism, or if Jesus (and scripture) still permits just retaliation, including just war ethics. Regardless of retaliation, the Genesis 9:6 passage emphasizes the importance and value of human life.

[8] Debate occurs about whether all suicides are premeditated. If they are not premediated, then can suicides be considered murder? Can there be mitigating circumstances that would designate suicides a variation of involuntary manslaughter or justifiable homicide? I maintain that people should not practice suicide, since it does violence toward one's relationship with God, the community, as well as with oneself.

[9] Although this passage refers to people in the plural being the "temple" of the Holy Spirit, it implies that people ought to care for their physical health as well as for the health of their souls and spirits.

[10] The writings of French neurologist Jean Charcot and psychiatrist Sigmund Freud left a legacy of schism between religion and mental health care. They viewed religion as a form of denying reality. Freud viewed belief in God as a projection of infantile wishes, an illusion, or a delusion. Both Charcot and Freud expressed personal animosity toward religion as a failed social

phenomenon that was unable to cure the insecurity and unhappiness of humanity.

[11] National Institute of Mental Health statistics from 2018 show that the rate of suicide is 3.7 times greater among males, and the rate of suicide attempts is greater among females. This phenomenon is most closely associated with methodology. The method or mode of suicidal behavior can impact the lethality of a suicide attempt. Women primarily attempt suicide by overdose or cutting. Men primarily attempt suicide by firearm or hanging. Overdose and cutting are less lethal than a gunshot or hanging. Access to lethal means also impacts the rate of suicide. These factors are most often cited in explaining why men die by suicide more than women.

[12] Fasting directly impacts our physical health and may require consultation with a medical professional. Missing a meal once a week may initially sound simple enough to manage, but there are multiple factors for us to consider. Medical conditions, insulin levels, heart rates, daily caloric requirements, hydration, and prescriptions must also be considered before starting a fast. Consider talking with clergy and a medical professional before engaging this practice.

[13] Specific studies mentioned were by De La Vega Sanchez, Park, Robins, and Stack. These four studies give the same conclusion that religion and spirituality lower suicide, suicidal behavior, and suicidal ideation.

About the Author

John Potter is an Army chaplain, a Christian pastor, and a Religion professor. He has pastored churches in the Midwest since 2002. John has overseas deployment experience and has conducted over 100 suicide interventions for service members, veterans, and military families. Chaplain Potter has served on the Governor's Behavioral Health Services Planning Council Suicide Prevention Subcommittee; the Governor's Challenge to Prevent Suicide for Service Members, Veterans, & Families Initiative; and the American Association of Suicidology's Military & Veteran Committee.

John is known for his scholarly acumen and pastor's heart. He is a popular suicide prevention trainer, speaker, and author who strongly believes that suicide is preventable, saving lives is possible, and that you can make a difference in the life of others.

John studied at Kansas State University and Nazarene Theological Seminary before earning a Doctor of Ministry degree in Spiritual Formation from Azusa Pacific Seminary.

www.ingramcontent.com/pod-product-compliance
Lightning Source LLC
Chambersburg PA
CBHW070922270326
41927CB00011B/2680